FROM THE FARTHER SHORE

Dear Elaine,
Because you also love
these shore and know,
so deeply, how to pay
attention.
Love,
Carol

FROM THE FARTHER SHORE
Discovering Cape Cod & the Islands Through Poetry

An Anthology
Edited by Alice Kociemba, Robin Smith-Johnson
& Rich Youmans

Bass River Press
in collaboration with
Calliope Poetry

From the Farther Shore
Edited by Alice Kociemba, Robin Smith-Johnson & Rich Youmans

Book design by Lauren Wolk
Cover Art by Mary Moquin

Printed by IngramSpark, Inc.

Published by Bass River Press, an imprint of The Cultural Center of Cape Cod
307 Old Main Street, South Yarmouth, Massachusetts 02664
www.cultural-center.org

Presented in collaboration with
Calliope Poetry
P.O. Box 1424, North Falmouth, MA 02556

Library of Congress Control Number: 2021941640

ISBN 978-0-578-79521-8

First Printing, 2021

Bass River Press and Calliope Poetry wish to thank the
South Yarmouth Library Association for its generous support.

TABLE OF CONTENTS

Leaving the Cape and Islands

Off Season: We Live Here

FROM THE EDITORS

For many visitors, the Cape and islands begin with a bridge.

At the northwest end of the Cape's flexed-arm peninsula, the Sagamore Bridge extends more than 600 feet over the Cape Cod Canal. Four miles southwest is the Bourne Bridge, a twin to the Sagamore with its arching, continuous truss. It also spans the canal, depositing visitors onto a rotary whose hub has been landscaped to spell "Cape Cod" in shrubbery.

Ever since they were constructed in the mid-1930s, the Bourne and the Sagamore bridges have been gateways, the prime connections from mainland Massachusetts to the idyllic "surf, sun, 'n fun" pleasures associated with Cape Cod and its neighboring islands, Martha's Vineyard and Nantucket. Millions of visitors cross those spans during the summer months, and tens of thousands continue to the island ferries in Woods Hole or Hyannis. Yes, the drive may take a while (particularly on traffic-clogged weekends), but to finally cross one of those bridges is to enter a different, more carefree world.

But, of course, that's not the whole story.

Like anywhere else, the region has had its share of historic episodes, colorful characters, notable landmarks, and traditions that have shaped generations of residents. Formed by ice sheets that spread and retreated, it was (and still is) the home of the Wampanoag, who have been in Massachusetts for more than 12,000 years. (The Mashpee Wampanoag and the Wampanoag Tribe of Gay Head [Aquinnah] are the only two federally recognized tribes in Massachusetts today.) The region also lured European settlers—the first, Bartholomew

Gosnold, provided an enduring name when he took on board "a great store of codfish"— and offered the first site of land to the Pilgrims after their voyage from England. The outer tip of the Cape has drawn many famous writers, poets, and artists attracted to the area's remoteness and quality of light, while world-renowned scientists still flock to Woods Hole, a bastion of marine biology and oceanography at the southwestern tip of the Cape. And although tourism now primarily drives the local economy, the Cape and islands have also been a home for thriving commercial fishermen and whalers, cranberry growers and pickers, and glassworks once renowned around the world.

There are indeed many facets to the Cape and islands, and we wanted to explore as many as we could through this anthology. We chose poetry as the vehicle for this journey because poems have a unique ability to transport a reader through time and space. They can render moments acutely and make even the commonplace seem new again. In a sense, they form their own bridges, and we knew that they would provide a deep understanding of and appreciation for this region that's beloved by so many.

When we set out on this project, we established a few guidelines for ourselves. First, we didn't want this book to be a collection of famous poets and poems—a "best of" so to speak. So many good poets have written about the Cape, including at least two U.S. laureates (Stanley Kunitz and Conrad Aiken, the latter of whom wrote the poem, "Mayflower," from which this anthology's title was taken). However, while we weren't averse to such famous entries (who would be?), we wanted to make sure the poems worked together to create a true sense of place. Rather than poems that offered only the poet's own thoughts and perspectives (which could have been set anywhere), we sought poems where the outer and interior landscapes melded and allowed the reader to experience the region for themselves. Poems imbued with the history, heritage, and spirit of the Cape and islands. Poems that could not have been set anywhere else.

Toward that end, we made lists of topics, locales, famous people, and historical moments identified with the Cape and islands, and used them as touchstones while we researched and solicited poems. And since we wanted to be as inclusive as possible, we put out both regional and national calls for poems—and received more than a thousand submissions.

Over the course of months, using those touchstones as our guides, we read and researched and read and debated and read and reconsidered and read some more. Above all, we were amazed at the response and the depth of both love and knowledge that had gone into so many of the poems. Hard decisions had to be made, especially in those cases when we had *too many* excellent pieces about a specific topic. Finally, after nearly a year, those thousand-plus submissions were winnowed down to the 118 you now hold in your hand. To replicate that feeling of an exploration, we've arranged the poems (somewhat) geographically, starting on the mainland—after all, part of the Cape and islands experience is actually in the approach. After taking some historical detours, the poems travel from one side of the Cape to the other and then over to Martha's Vineyard and Nantucket. The journey ends with a brief section about leaving the Cape and islands (another part of the experience) and then a coda: "Off Season: We Live Here" looks at the often hardscrabble lives of the population that *doesn't* leave when the days turn colder and the streets become more deserted. Days when the quiet can also be savored.

For guides, you'll find a wide range of voices, from the well known to those just gaining recognition, but all exhibit a true appreciation for the Cape and islands. They explore its history and heritage, its natural beauty, and even those aspects (overdevelopment, drug abuse) that don't make the travel brochures but are also a part of the region's history. And if you want to discover more, the end of the anthology offers a section of notes that flesh out some of the topics explored.

And now, it's time to begin the exploration. We hope, through these poems, you can revisit favorite locations and memories, and maybe even make new discoveries. Above all, we hope the anthology serves as a bridge to a deeper understanding of what has made the Cape and islands so iconic, and why their legacy still endures.

Alice Kociemba, Robin Smith-Johnson, Rich Youmans

TO THE CAPE

STANLEY KUNITZ

Route Six

The city squats on my back.
I am heart-sore, stiff-necked,
exasperated. That's why
I slammed the door,
that's why I tell you now,
in every house of marriage
there's room for an interpreter.
Let's jump into the car, honey,
and head straight for the Cape,
where the cock on our housetop crows
that the weather's fair,
and my garden waits for me
to coax it into bloom.
As for those passions left
that flare past understanding,
like bundles of dead letters
out of our previous lives
that amaze us with their fevers,
we can stow them in the rear
along with ziggurats of luggage
and Celia, our transcendental cat,
past-mistress of all languages,
including Hottentot and silence.
We'll drive non-stop till dawn,
and if I grow sleepy at the wheel,
you'll keep me awake by singing
in your bravura Chicago style
Ruth Etting's smoky song,
"Love Me or Leave Me,"

belting out the choices.

Light glazes the eastern sky
over Buzzards Bay.
Celia gyrates upward
like a performing seal,
her glistening nostrils aquiver
to sniff the brine-spiked air.
The last stretch toward home!
Twenty summers roll by.

LINDSAY KNOWLTON

Wanting

Riding down, as a kid,
on the route that ran you through Middleboro
where the outlaw Coyle Brothers hid
and sun-dazed turtles still made their muzzy
pilgrimage across the cracked tarmac;
then stopping once for sandwiches, once for gas,
once to water the panting dogs,
and then riding again;
it seemed in the day's shimmering haze
that Buzzard's Bay was a mirage,
that you would never reach
Wareham's Gateway to Cape Cod, and—just up ahead,
just around the bend—the best store of all!
Even then, traffic at a crawl, inching (creeping!) along,
The Mill Pond Diner, Pelican Package,
Katie Palm Reader, and Tina Nipa's Basketry;
still—heavy lidded, head tipping, but before the Bridge,
righted by the whiff of fried clams and now, finally—
Seabreeze Gifts, where if this time
your father was relaxed and feeling flush,
if this time he would ignore
your mother's dismissal of shell art
and pallid pectined jellies,
you could lose yourself in rows of ducks and geese which,
you knew,
would never clear Onset or the shores of Buttermilk Bay
but which because they were new,
because they were freshly painted red,
and blue and green,

because please you needed one anyway,
but if the answer should be "no,"
categorically "NO" to the most scaled-down
hack facsimile of brant or mallard,
then poor second-best:
the first sullen mouth-watering pick
of the pastel salt-water taffies.

ALICE KOCIEMBA

Bourne Bridge

Not the hard rain
the rivers crave,
not the downpour
to quench the forest floor,
just a light mist,
on almost empty roads,
as I'm entombed in grey,
the only sound—
an intermittent shush—
wipers clearing windshield;
this quiet is pleasing,
a monochromatic alone,
when suddenly the overcast
lightens from charcoal to dove,
then splits into strands
of mauve, salmon, rose,
and the bridge ahead, luminous,
wrapped in a pale blue shawl,
each raindrop clings,
glistening in pure light
that's always there
even when hidden—
I've come home.

ORIGIN STORIES

RICH YOUMANS

Doane Rock

A glacial erratic in Eastham, MA, and the largest exposed boulder on Cape Cod.

Taller than three men,
its granite face all lumps and ridges,
folds and furrows, as if formed
by a hand that once held the sun…

shadowed by pitch pine and oak,
sunk deep as an eyetooth
into this sandy soil, into layers
of gneiss and gabbro and diorite—
debris of an ice sheet that pushed and scoured
and tugged this terrain into a spit
that now arcs like a shaking fist…

Think of it.

20,000 years ago, the Laurentide
creaked and cracked southward,
carrying a cargo of boulders from
Canada and the Gulf of Maine,
then retreated, leaving nothing
but upheaval:
moraines and their erratic mounds;
outwash plains braided
by meltwater; ice chunks
sunk into the soil like
depth charges;
and half-buried boulders

shouldering into sunlight.

Like this one,

which inhabits space so thoroughly
that everything moves around it,
slows to a glacial pace. I reach out to
touch its coarse face, its topography
of lichen, its moist hollows.
I press my palm into its ancient ruts
and, for a moment, am in a time
when ice cleaved the Earth,
when sun-splintering white filled the eye,
and sang as if in chains.

SUSAN R. HORTON

White Girl Enters Indian Lands

For Marcus Hendricks

"What was this land called before white people came,"
Native American historian Vine DeLoria was asked.
"Ours," he said.

Yesterday, before we entered Dennis woods,
you told us your people knew
the ground we were standing on
        as Turtle Island.

Yesterday, you sang the chant
your people had sung to reassure
all the creatures living in these woods
that those about to enter meant them no harm.

But before chanting the words taught you
by your 92-year-old grandmother so recently lost,
you planted your feet wide and solid on the earth,
looked out over the high pines
and the cooper's hawk flying there,
gathered your spirit, connected it with hers,
and began to sing the song of your ancestors.

But before beginning, out of respect you'd
removed the cap that had hidden your hair
during our winter treks, so for the first time,
I saw your ebony hair gleaming in the morning sun,
as that of your Nipmuc and Wampanoag forebears had

as they set out in their mishoons to gather fish
          from their weirs ·
to bring to their families' summer wetos
in the dunes near Stage Harbor
in what we now call Chatham,
or, as winter came on, to lead them
along the sandy paths running
along Pleasant Bay, to long-homes
          in the sheltering hollows of Orleans' deep woods.

Four hundred years later, you are
as much a knower of nature as they,
          and as brave.
As they walked paths through lands
that were theirs, and did not fear,
you lead us, bushwhacking our way
along the paths of our unknowingness.
Invite us to feel the presence of the ancients,
forever here, and very near. Katabatas.

MARY CLARE CASEY

Fireball at the Powwow

Before the teams are divided,
there is ritual. First the tearing of sheets,
the wrapping and layering,
hand over hand until the ball is formed.
Then the careful placing of wire
to keep all that has been created in place.
Finally, the ball is soaked in kerosene,
that liquid fire, to make it burn
with the sun's heat. When the game begins
wind rushes across the field;
some say it is the feet of ancestors
who have come to carry others across time.
The players whisper their names:
Good Running, Long Arrow, Blue Hawk,
Giant Rabbit. The fireball flies
through darkness, sparks falling
silent as feathers to the ground.

RICH YOUMANS

This Language, This Blood, This Land

"My blood and bones come from the very land that you know as Mashpee." —Jessie Little Doe Baird, from an oversight hearing conducted by the U.S. Senate Commission on Indian Affairs about "Examining Efforts to Maintain and Revitalize Native Languages for Future Generations."

This language resides deep in our blood,
these nouns move and breathe
like bucks in green brush, or stay
still as pond water, absorbing sky.

This language once delivered Genesis,
the Bible's stern tales, and showed
the theft of fertile land, when a tribe
lost its footing and fell down

and now rises again, after the dreams
in which the old voices called for
a new generation to reconnect

with why the pines stay green,
with the breath of cattail reeds,
with this language that falls
from the tongue like starlight
of centuries past,

onto a land
that is us.

BRENDAN GALVIN

Names by a River

The keels of the *Speedwell* and *Discoverer*
four hundred years ago passed over
where I am walking among the glasswort
and hudsonia this morning, the river's
estuary here then. Before Bradford
and Miles Standish you came
with fifty men in armor out of Bristol,
barely a man yourself, nevertheless
Captain Martin Pring, from your portrait
I'd say a handy little dude like Standish
and John Smith, your chin-beard sharp
as a poinado. Enough mitten-shaped leaves
of the sassafras here to make a homeward cargo
for both holds, you calculated—a possible cure
for the French pox. A kingbird works
the dune grasses for insects this morning,
at what you named Whitson Bay after
a prime investor in your voyage.

All that is left of 1603 has been shifted,
wind and sea, ground down, sorted, re-pummeled,
blown sideways, sea and wind, processed and
overlain with grasses and snows among the vagaries
of the river, itself renamed: Pamet now for the tribe
you pressed into flight with the mastiffs
Gallant and Fool. After a few thousand walks
among the nesters here, I call these dunes
and flats Egg Island, in part to confuse
the local hiking club, identical in their

baggy shorts and yellow t-shirts, their catalog
explorer hats, outfits absurd as those you gifted
the natives with, those "divers sorts of
meanest merchandise."

Who do I think I am, since only change
is unchanging here: Whitson's Bay
to Egg Island, and your Mount Aldworth
to Tom's Hill, after a last Pamet
who lived up there? Even the French pox
has run through a litany of names,
not many as impugning, but all as colorful,
the Grandgore, the Black Lion,
and the sassafras itself went into
root beer. You stayed seven weeks, then sailed
from the August heat inimical to northern blood.

Since mariners read the birds, though
you wouldn't have names for some, no doubt
you saw the flocks dropping down
and reforming for the south, semipalmated
plovers this morning, big name for a brief
flash of white with half-webbed feet,
their migration begun, but you didn't
stay on for the grand transitions—
a stray albatross, wing-broken, rolled over
the dunes in a January blow, or the way
a north wind surprises a walker as he faces
about into it. Pilgrims, briefly, converting
to whalers, then trap fishermen—would you
have called them *Portingales?*—
and the fish houses, ice houses, coal-fired freights,
and the river forever trying new entries and
departures between Corn Hill and Fisher's Beach,
scouring its bed into sandbars, undermining,

making runs up the valley, trying to join
the Atlantic at the farther shore.

And here, as I read the flats this morning,
going side-by-side with a set of tracks, a dog
at first, but no mastiff: feet too narrow,
heel pads flat at the back, and no splay,
so more likely a coyote, perhaps one of those
you called "dogs with sharp and long noses."
The names never stick, as if in the naming
the thing itself is changed. These whorls
in the riverbed could be the fingerprint of God,
and the slow motion whip-cracks of the river
keep flexing over time between headlands.

BRENDAN GALVIN

Pitch Pines

Some trees loft their heads
like symmetrical green bells,
but these, blown one-sided
by winds salted out of the northeast,
seem twisted from the germ.
Not one will lean the same way as another.

Knotted but soft, they mingle
ragged branches and rot to punkwood,
limbs flaking and dying
to ribs, to antlers and spidery twigs,
scaly plates slipping off the trunks.

Hanging on, oaks rattle maroon clusters
against winter. But these, resinous in flues,
blamed for a history of cellar holes,
snap in the cold and fall
to shapes like dragons asleep,

or thin out by dropping sour needles
on acid soil. For one week in May
they pollinate windows, a shower
that curdles water to golden scum.

From Bartholomew Gosnold's deck,
Brereton saw this cape timbered to its shores
with the hardwoods that fell to keels
and ribbing, to single meetinghouse beams
as long as eight men.

Stands of swamp cedar, cleared for cranberries,
were split to shakes or cut lengthwise
for foundations, while sheep cropped
elm and cherry sprouts
and plows broke the cleancut fields.

Fifty cords at a time, birch and maple
melted bog iron in pits; elm and beech
boiled the Atlantic to its salts; red oak
fired the glassworks at Sandwich—

till the desert floundered
out of the backlands and knocked
on the rear doors of towns
and this peninsula drifted
in brushfire haze,

and, clenching their cones
under crown fires, the grandfathers
of these pines held on until
heat popped their seeds
to the charred ground.

ELIZABETH BRADFIELD

On the Magnetism of Certain Spots on Earth, Like Provincetown

> *Governor Bradford's wife, Dorothy, was drowned in the harbor....*
> *It would seem that the God of the infidels, which they call chance,*
> *had a hand in this mysterious jumble.*
> > —*Time and the Town,* Mary Heaton Vorse

November. But still the wild light bounced
between sand and sky, uncultured. It was pulling her
apart,
      unlacing what held her.

            Wind did its part.
    Burrowing, pushing
grains of the new world into her seams, chafing there, rubbing
until the cloth couldn't hold.

              An accident, then, not fate or
God's will, her fall out of air's strange freedoms.
She had begun, you see, even on the rough journey over,
     even in the dark hold of the ship,
to believe in chance.

       Chance that this spit
curled them, chance that the sun, just moments ago,
hit the dunes hard and came to her prayer-like,

as if all her other prayers had been just mumblings,
shadows rather than light.

      There should be a word

22

for what I've come to, she thought as waves made her the first to see

that elsewhere, anywhere, was worth casting off from
in order to land here, in order to come to even this rest.

SUSAN DONNELLY

Thoreau's Cape Cod

Death's is the long arm
that reaches across the book. Over his tramp
through the pulling sands of Nauset,
beneath his catalogues of beach pea and spurge,
the carcass lies
tossed onto the shore.

He had seven more years. The ocean took such time
over its catch! "There is no telling
what it might not vomit up."
Cods full of nutmegs,
a bottle "stopp'd tight and half-full of red ale,"
towcloth, turnip seed,
and a lost anchor
that "sunken faith and hope of mariners."

The Cape's arm reached toward something
beyond land. A fisted curve,
with the smack of the unpredictable Atlantic
coming up against its outside.
And what the fist tried to hold
fell through in grains
as every year changed
the shape of the beaches.
What is in Provincetown dexterous ladies
"emptied their shoes at each step"?
There was nothing

constant
as his own deep pond.
Massachusetts Bay
was a maw of foundered ships,
a death's cradle of immigrants,
slung back and forth with a stark rocking,
that tore from them
their poor clogs and lockets,
threw them to purify
into pale ivory on its beaches.

It was the leaping ground
of the Howling Whale
that all the little boats hounded to shore,

to render from each
a hundred-dollar barrel of oil,

then leave them,
opened and rotting,
warning off walkers with their stink.

> "The annals of this voracious beach!
> Who could write them?"

Against the glass
of even the Highland Light
"nineteen small yellowbirds"
broke their necks one night.

Back home in Concord, he walked always to the West,
sniffed out a new trail each day.

Here with "all America behind him,"
a man could stumble for hours over the dunes

and die at last
in a charity hut,
one arm outstretched to the cold hearth.

SCENES FROM
THE CAPE & ISLANDS

SARA LETOURNEAU

At the Sandwich Glass Museum

Every hour, on the hour, the glassblower
dons his protective sleeve and readies his tools
at the museum's furnace, a freestanding brick pillar
that could be mistaken for a chimney.
In front of a crowd of thirty, a class from the local
elementary school, he introduces himself,
explains where the glass nuggets come from
and what he's going to make, but not how he'll make it.
The students and teacher nod, rapt despite
sweat beading on their foreheads.
After all, they're here to learn the "how."

He takes the pipe, one end immersed
in the furnace's 2,000-degree heat, and reaches
deeper inside to the crucible of molten glass.
Out he draws his first gather, pearlike and comet-white,
kept on center by his constant spinning of the pipe,
his fingers turning the rod as deftly
as a spinner spinning wool into yarn.
He blows a breath through the pipe's cool end,
trapping air inside the glass so it inflates,
then sits at his bench and shapes the swell
with the closed blades of his jacks so it's
smooth and symmetrical.

Back and forth, the glassblower
moves from the glory hole to reheat the glass;
to his bench, where he sculpts it
with his jacks and a water-soaked block,

sparks flying like fireflies, steam rising from the contact;
to his feet again, to blow more breath into
his incandescent bulb, or to "let it run," pointing the pipe
downward so gravity can elongate the honey-lava
with its bare, unseen hands,
and once to coat it in cobalt-blue frit.
His movements all the while mimic a dancer's:
fluid, deliberate, expertly timed, choreographed
over years of training in this ancient, Syrian-invented craft.

Eventually, at his bench, he uses his shears to cut,
jacks to ply, and tweezers the size of kitchen tongs
to twist and tease the glass into its final form.
And in these climactic movements, history comes full-circle,
each motion paying tribute
to Deming Jarves, the Boston & Sandwich Glass Company,
and all the master craftsmen who brought their delicate,
igneous art with them from as far away
as England and Ireland.

All of these lessons are reinforced
in the museum's exhibits and glassware collections.
Yet none of them will draw the same delighted gasps
from the audience as the glassblower's newest creation:
a whelk shell veined in blue, so lifelike
it could have been plucked from Town Neck Beach,
just over a mile away.

DONNA RAZETO

On Selling the Cottage in Sandwich Downs

after Stephen Berg

if they ask if you can hear
the sound of the ocean from the house
tell them about the dunes
the lullaby of grasses
tell them about the wind
its humming corners
ask them which rifled grain of sand
blows these last footsteps into the marsh
ask them who then
steps onto the beach at low tide
silence for breath
to call the ocean in

WINSTON BOLTON

A Summer Life

Falmouth, MA, 9/26/1990

He pumps awhile, then rakes.
The water, golden brown,
turns black with mud,
and from the bottom come

the white, solid, living stones.
He tells us "take some"—
some of the few he's gathered
in a morning's work.

Out here, clamming,
he has one bare handhold
on existence. A summer life.
Like a climber clinging

to rock, who lugs himself
aloft—up sheer stone—
grinning at the sun,
never looking down.

LAUREL KORNHISER

Abandoned Bog, West Falmouth

The pump house is shuttered,
the stream sunk to late-summer lows.

Shin-high in the drying grasses
dragonflies flicker.

"Souls of the dead," say the reverent.

Creatures of carpe diem,
they fracture sunlight in flight.

Promethean, they strike teal matchheads
against the flint of my eye until I see

a weathered-gray pump house
hiding a primed well,

a mottled brook engaged
to a pure pond just beyond,

the brown peat conspiring
with coarse sand and gravel

to create crimson berries
ready to be raised.

KATHLEEN CASEY

The Knob at Quissett Harbor

It invites all to enter.
An unlatched timber gate
bordered by boulders.

Sun flickers over the root-surfaced path,
which twists and turns
around scrub pine and oak.

Now warblers with sun-colored throats.
We forget shadows that dull our journey.

By bracken and beach plum bushes,
sky meets bay with overwhelming
blue. We breathe

and breathe again.

DANIEL TOBIN

Quissett

The sun on the water is an open palm.
Saw-grass stills its lances on the sand.
The boats are nodding in a heavy calm.

This scene could be an otherworldly balm.
Bright hulls trace their colors to the strand.
The sun on the water is an open palm.

The gulls themselves have given up alarm
And float suspended in windless air and
The boats are nodding in a heavy calm.

No swells, no surge, no dissonance of storm
Drumming bluntly from offing to the land:
The sun on the water is an open palm

That gestures without moving, no quest or qualm,
Just stillness, insistent—its soft command.
The boats are nodding in a heavy calm

That feels like the notion inside a psalm,
Lightness lifting everything like a hand.
The sun on the water is an open palm.
The boats are nodding in a heavy calm.

MARY SWOPE

Waking, Woods Hole

Nobska Beach

Enter this clear morning like a swimmer,
dive into its perfect wave:
mares' tails sweep the sky on a north wind
above the dark Sound, crisp with sails.
Past those stiff triangles, ferries throb and cross,
frothed at the bow, foam-waked,
headed for islands that shape our horizon.

What the eye hungers for, lungs take in—
great gulps of morning, the laundered sky-smell.
Joggers move up the hill toward the lighthouse
rejoicing in easy limbs. You too
can dive in, enter the touching air,
or, left behind some wall or sealed window,
miss out on the fanfare of morning.

FRANK FINALE

At the Edge of the Sea with Rachel Carson

Woods Hole, summer of '29.
"A delightful place to biologize,"
you declare in a letter to a friend. Woods Hole,
where you came *magna cum laude*
to the red-brick MBL. A town where
"One can't walk very far in any direction
without running into water."

Today, I sit by the bronze statue of you
staring out to sea, a sense of wonder
in our gaze. Your mother taught you
to look at nature closely, to walk in a sea
of woods, to feel the trees, the fairyland lichen,
to smell the soil in different months; nudged you
to look up on a summer night at millions
of stars that blazed in darkness.

In sea wind, you wrote books that sailed
to faraway places with their cargo of words.
Now I sit with you before the town awakens.
Fishing boats nudge the wooden docks,
Vineyard Sound sparkles with miniature suns.
Gulls sail and cry. I draw a deep breath,
lift my eyes in praise.

LINDA PASTAN

At Woods Hole

site of the Marine Biological Laboratory

To measure the straight line of a mast,
the angle of wave, dune, spread sail
is all the geometry of this shore—
and the shark's fin on its way to kill
bisecting the arc of a half-moon
on its way to sea.

A sunfish tacking into the wind
or the gull dropping a locked clam
on ledges of rock below
is the psychology of this shore;
and the edge of the sea unravelling
from here to Hatteras
all of its history.

And we learn nothing, lying
on sand hot and pliant as each other's flesh,
making our promises while rows of cars gleam
in the distance like beached mackerel,
and waves seem to bring the water in forever
even as the tide moves surely out.

TRICIA KNOLL

Squid Jigging in Woods Hole

The quiet man in jeans hits the jetty
after a beer at the bar.
His favorite lure is a luminescent pink
fantasy squid jig. He sits
on a white five-gallon bucket.
Wharf lights dim the stars.

Two men and a woman speak Vietnamese.
They know what they are doing,
especially the lady who smiles,
without words, bouncing her styled jig.

They teach him.
The squid rise to high light,
cephalopod moon call.

He delivers the squid to me later,
milky gray in his ink-filled bucket,
squid big as thumbs.

He trims, chops, cuts
and stir-fries the calimari, leaving
squid slime with eyes like BB's
open in kitchen spotlights.

I eat calimari, sure I do, but
those eyes in my garbage pail,
the lid shut tight.
Rock-hard black baby eyes.

CLIFF SAUNDERS

Penikese Island Triptych

*Note: From 1905 to 1921, the state of Massachusetts maintained
a small leper colony on Penikese Island.*

I. First Night on the Island (November 1905)

A chill sweeps across the porch
of his cottage. The temperature

seems to plunge fifteen degrees
in a matter of seconds. Peering

into the blue-black firmament,
he sees faint fingers of fog streaking

over the shoreline and above the cottage.
He stares at the pitch-black sea,

at a world with no light, with no hope.
At that moment, he feels as if he

is being buried alive within a mausoleum
of fog, weightless but no less suffocating.

II. Encounter with Halley's Comet (April 1910)

With field glasses in hand, he stands
atop the island's lone hill on a gusty night,

scanning a moonless sky full of stars

for the fabled visitor. Gazing to the north,

he spots the "wandering star" and leaps
up and down a few times in triumph.

"At last!" he cries, staring at the object
through his binoculars. To him it resembles

a tiny fish of light. Suddenly he wants to be
that solitary comet streaming across the night sky.

He can't be free as the comet is. And that's what he—
what every patient on Penikese—wants: to be free.

III. Death of a Fellow Patient (December 1914)

On the day of his housemate's passing, flurries
drift to the ground all day and expire on impact.

Slowly, inexorably, snowflakes flutter down
like tiny remnants of a spirit that has disintegrated

during its ascent, as if unprepared to depart
the material world. The sea takes on a cast

of milky glass throughout the day. Its gentle waves
lap mere inches from the trembling hand

of a starfish stranded at water's edge. Patiently
the starfish awaits the tide's return, and soon

it is taken back into the folds of its mother.
A seagull circles soundlessly above the island.

ELIZABETH BRADFIELD

A Further Explication of Irony

Penikese Island, 1973

Another night on this island you could steal away from, given ice
or jet pack. Mainland clear in good weather but too far
by crawl or backstroke. You're a boy. Thirteen. Fifteen.

You've done something to be sent here. Petty
theft, knife fights, worse. Nights, you can't help it,
you think of the lepers, scabby and shuffling, here

before it was a school. You can almost
hear them. No traffic. No fathers. No dogs
rattling chain link as you walk their alleys. But still,

sounds. Wind, mostly. Waves. The scrabble of mice. Then,
mid-summer, a new noise, half mutter, half scuffle.
And I bet you could give a shit about ecology,

demography, or much of anything beyond getting out or
getting up the pecking order so that nights,
at least, you could sleep instead of listen. Did you

know there are birds that spend their lives at sea?
Once a year they're forced in to nest, so find the smallest,
most isolated shore, make secret flights to and from

a burrow at the edges of light, exchange odd conversations
in darkness. At sea their wings nearly slice the wave caps.
You've never seen such delight in soaring.

This is what I envy: you were there. You
slept lightly and heard a rustle gone at daybreak.
Your old stone walls were thick enough to be fissured

and yet still sound. Why did you tell?
And why did that teacher listen to you and then
listen with you at night? How did he know

to recognize a sound he'd never heard? You found
Manx shearwaters nesting in Massachusetts.
None of the books knew about this yet. Those birds

were truants, using what's almost abandoned.
For them, your exile was refuge.

SAMM CARLTON

Salt Song

Cut out along one horizon
our ocean slips on currents
through holes close-set as eyelets
between the Elizabeth Islands,
a chant of names:

Nonamesset, Uncatena, Great Naushon
and Nashawena, Cuttyhunk, Penikese,
the little Weepeckets, and Pasque.

Heaving up whale-like
to the south,
and blocking my view of England
is Martha's Vineyard.

Small white sails poke
along its shore,
and out there somewhere
lost in the mist,
Nantucket.

I close my eyes and sing to my younger self
listening to the echo.
Nonamessett, Uncatena,
Great Naushon and Nashawena.

In between are memories
jumbled by tide and waves:
family, summer friends, lovers,

births, boats, badminton,
marriages, swimming,
death.

I lie flattened on the sand.
Deep currents change places:
comfort, discomfort, pleasure, pain.
Unknown voices swirl, people sun,
their children dig, swim, run

as this afternoon on Nobska,
like so many decades
and countless days before,
rolls down,
pulls away.

Nonamesset, Great Naushon.

JEFFREY HARRISON

Returning to Cuttyhunk

I've heard half a dozen meanings for the name
and none of them alike. To me it always seemed
a baby's nickname for a baby island:
a low, scruffy hill on the horizon,
so small it looks as if the windmill on it
might lift it off the ocean like a seaplane.

That day the Sunday *Globe* said it meant "Go away,"
and I believed it. I thought they must have turned
the windmill on like an electric fan,
a wind machine that blew the whitecaps off
the green reptilian waves, into our faces.
We gave up and tacked into Sakonnet.

After the storm blew over, we tried again.
We spotted Cuttyhunk. At first the cliffs
of Gay Head looked like part of it. The windmill
stood there in the middle, without waving
its arms, and stared at us inscrutably.
The Gosnold monument was over to the right,

like a lonely chess rook in its corner
waiting for the most strategic moment
to castle with the windmill-king.
The harbor on the other side looked like
a plate full of hors d'oeuvres, bristling with toothpicks.
Then we saw the gray, Monopoly-sized houses.

When we sailed past tiny, treeless Penikese

(a former leper colony and now
a bird sanctuary), the waves were so smooth—
more like a lake's than an ocean's—it was
as if the thinnest film of mist were on them,
softening the blues and oranges of sunset.

We docked near the fish shacks, then walked up the road
between two blooming hedges: the island
took us in its arms (privet, milkweed,
honeysuckle, multiflora rose).
The evening air seemed hazy from the pollen.
I said, "It's happening, the island's taking off."

We walked along a dry stone wall with orange
lichen on it, like spilled paint, dried and cracked,
and past a little church whose weather vane
was a striped bass, wide-eyed and open-mouthed
as if astonished by the clouds above him
which looked like pink cabbages in a blue field.

JARITA DAVIS

Harvesting a Return

Over and over again, owners and overseers of cranberry bogs
pronounce the Cape Verder, whether he picks by hand, scoop or snap,
the very best harvester of cranberries on the Cape Cod bogs.
          Albert Jenks, anthropologist, 1924

I can look at the cranberries, yes, but not eat them. It's their color that's sweet
when the pink beads and candied crimson pebbles tumble into their wooden boxes.

If you buy your own land, in three to five years you can harvest a full crop.
In three years, I'll be in Fogo again, telling my sobrinhos stories of the bog.

Not about arthritis snapping my hips and ankles as I crouch in the dewy dawn,
or the skin splitting my hand as I reach from the cold, dry air into the wet vines.

I'll bring back different stories, American clothes, and a handful of cranberries
for each child. I'll laugh when they spit the bitter flesh back into their hands.

When their faces gather, scattered brown layers eclipsing each other, I'll tell how here
parents picked and scooped and told children stories of Nho Lobo, the lazy wolf.

How women picked too. Mothers in wide-brimmed hats stained their dresses
while kneeling on crushed leaves and cranberries in the wet bogs, teaching

their children those old Criole songs: the one about the rooster
who longs for his youth, wishing he could fly. And how the children helped,

stumbling under the awkward empty wooden crates, gray and
bigger than themselves, and brought them to their parents, bent in the bogs.

I'll tell them about autumn tumbling behind boxes of cranberries set at the edge
of the fields and how the end of each day would fall from the hills with a quiet fire

of trees like narrow volcanoes exploding orange and yellow leaves. The evenings
folded with the smell of burning wood, as colors collapsed into the sunset.

How all through September and October and November, late into every Saturday
night, we sang along with the accordions and mandolins in cabins by the bogs.

We danced, and the children took warm bread with cranberry jam from their mothers'
rough hands, hands torn by the berries' vine and stained red beneath the nail.

Work on the bog is work that makes you feel old. Old enough to wonder how
you are still bending your back over another man's crops, not your own.

My scoop snaps across the vines' twigs. The money comes slowly, but it comes.
Boxes stand stacked, bulging with berries. If the picking is good this year, and next,

I'll bring an aching armload of stories and berries back from the fiery fields
of this other Cape to those brown faces in the beige mountains of Fogo.

ALICE KOCIEMBA

Death of Teaticket Hardware

I never knew his name,
nor he mine.
He was always there.
Patient. Polite. Shy.

I never knew the name of what I needed, either.
But he did. After listening.
"You know that thingamajig
that connects the hose to the washer."
"I need the innards of a lamp."

He'd find it in a flash—
through overcrowded aisles,
so narrow only a munchkin could maneuver.
In the back of the store, on the dusty top shelf
where whatsits live.

He'd tell me how to use it.
And he'd tell me again,
drawing it on the little scratch pad
he kept at the register (not the electric kind)
next to the dish of pennies
and the bowl of lollipops.
I would always leave with a red one,
        and confidence.

He was the kindest man in town.

I imagined he went home at 5:30 every night

to the apartment above the store,
and told his wife over meatloaf and mashed potatoes,
green beans and pecan pie:
"That lady came in again today, seems bright enough
but doesn't even know a lamp has a socket."
And he'd smile when she would say, "Oh, Mrs. Dimwit."
And they would turn on the News at Six.

The drive to town is eerie now
that Teaticket Hardware is gone.
Boarded-up windows stare like a zombie
whose soul's been stolen by Wal-Mart.

Peter Cabral, son of John, son of Peter, son of John,
I never said hello, or goodbye, or thank you.

J. LORRAINE BROWN

Alone on Sage Lot Pond

After all, this should be the perfect day:
the sky is blue mist
hanging over the marsh,
and morning sun scatters
scraps of light
waking pickleweed
and buttercup.
I tip my face
in the plummy warmth.
Blackbirds wear hearts
on their wings. Ducks
on the path preen
gilt-green feathers
smooth as Baltic amber.
Only one swan stirs the pond,
the curve of her neck so tempting
I could pluck it like a harp.

ROBIN SMITH–JOHNSON

My Son at Four, Walking South Cape Beach

Gathering shells in late spring
is a small task—
each tucked in his palm,

some to be stored away
in the blue bucket,
others thrown back.

No one had to show him
the art of discerning
one from another:

conch, razor, slipper shell.
Even the curious half-light,
sun hidden by a sudden cloud,

illuminates that moment of decision—
what catches his eye,
what means.

DAVID R. SURETTE

Kennedy Compound, Hyannis Port

My grandfather ran an elevator
parking garage in Winthrop Square.
He knew all the chauffeurs in town,
saw every local celebrity pass through:
senators, actors, ball players. Presidents.

The Kennedy's chauffeur snuck us all in once
to see the Marine helicopter land.
We waited by the bright green lawn.

I saw her pony.
Then I saw her.

Against the roaring engine and slashing blades,
the president stepped out, bent over, arms extended.
Five feet away, Caroline skipped toward him.
The father-child embrace froze
the moment, made it larger than my world.

I was seven years old and swore undying love.

And then this man, her father, was dead
and my whole neighborhood wept.
I was only seven years old
and had not yet learned to weep.

I still saw her pony,
the way she skipped toward him.
I filled the hours with rescue fantasies,
a world with greater meaning than my own.

ROBIN SMITH–JOHNSON

Gale Warnings

Hyannis Harbor

Wind and rain blow misgivings
into the faces of strangers
struggling with umbrellas down Main Street.

At the harbor under a sunken sky,
gulls squall over whitecaps,
swept aside in salt spray.

Skiffs rise and fall in the wake
of a departing ferry. Lines
creak against the pilings;

there's a smell of fish and brine,
the rain quickens.
The edges of things bleed

outside the frame.
This is how a poem enters:
by making silence larger.

SUSAN DONNELLY

The Law Ghosts

—The Barnstable House

The old house, now law offices,
has at least five ghosts.
One is a girl child, drowned,
it is said, in the river
the house was built over.
A whiskered elder in frock coat
looks down now and then
from an oriel window.
There's a hanged man
by the old stables, a closet
where some can hear singing.
And going home autumn nights
from the titles and felonies,
you might meet the beautiful,
black-haired woman who
wrings her hands on the landing.

DEIRDRE CALLANAN

E Is for Edward

Above the Cinema's cloth-clad chairs,
your ghost floats past Kent's swirls & stars,
drifts to the aisle. In Converse high-tops,
paperback tucked in your jeans' pocket,
you sift to a side row, hover near
Helen & Herb as images scroll the screen…

You as fixture at Balanchine's ballets, decade after decade.
Strawberry Lane's books, finials, iron utensils, art,
among which cats nestle in countless nooks.

In your car's back seat, polar bears await
your daily drive to Jack's, your counter stool;
when Eve & John mention a young girl's
birthday, just like that, on a three-inch square
you sketch a feisty, squint-eyed cat, sign,
"For Samantha   Edward Gorey."

Asked to design an invitation,
you decline payment but
from Gillette pen & Pelican ink,
two giddy cats emerge, toss yarn
into sailors' love knots.

On Cape—puppets, caprices, whimsy.
In New York, your Dracula set stuns.
One after another, the books—
first text, then drawings'
meticulous crosshatches, multiple patterns:

Twenty-six hapless youngsters
squashed, smothered, struck.
In fur coats & ample scarves,
Edna & co. pump a handcar
into a tunnel. On the far side of Iron Hill,
readers still wait for them to emerge…

Credits roll over a backdrop of Loplop's cousin—
our mouse-nibbled Figbash—
de-stuffed & disfigured yet still endearing,
his shadowy-shapery reminds us of you.

PAULA TRESPAS

Union Street Bog, Yarmouth

I walk into the painting.
The sunlit cranberry bog
circled by a moat not determined by tide
shimmers with every whim of wind.
Its boundaries, tufted by wild buttercup
only last week, now breed clover,
their globe heads, hair-styled purple and punk,
poke from spiky patches of grass.
Tendrils of wild grapevine curlicue
into my space. Hapless blackberry
vines entwine and tangle in the under grasses,
their petals white as pearls on a wedding veil.

A sturdy old Cape Codder, making his rounds
as he's done for countless springs,
carries a walking stick tall and weathered as he.
He removes his cap stenciled with the Florida
place he visits each winter and, holding its visor,
strokes back his thinning gray hair.

"See that poison ivy over there?" He points a crooked
finger toward a clump of menacing weed.
"This bog's a goner."

He doesn't notice that my shoulders slump.
I avert my eyes, concentrating on clover.

SUSAN NISENBAUM BECKER

Passionate Attraction

Light slides along slabs of the Bass River
broken by our sandballs and pebbles
into lozenges of sun, concentrics racing
back to us standing wet-footed in sweetflag.
At 14 months Olivia stumbles
into who she's just becoming.
Hearing *croak, croak*, she lifts herself
from the business of sticks and rocks,
tastes of mud and rust water—she still eats
the world. She spots the fishing heron
statue-still, stilts planted on a watery plinth,
neck winding to its dagger-head
poised to thrust. Sudden rising
legs tucked beneath its body's cape—
it is its own spear plunging into fiery maples.
She turns to me, bumps her hands together,
sign for *more*. Would that I could
replay for her that lift, that arc,
that vanishing.

PHYLLIS HENRY–JORDAN

Over the Shoal, Bass River

"I'm pushing you off now, Puss;
grab the tiller,
pull in the sheet,
push down the centerboard
once you're off the shoal."

I watch with alarm and
wonder the widening water
between my sail and the shore
that was my father.

I wanted back the land;
how could I know that the water
would become as familiar as
the hollows of my hand?

Along a disappearing shoreline
sandpipers were fast retreating
in their trot along the beach,
running close to every wave,
hoping for one to cast up a
breakfast within their skittish reach.

Far from sight now their footprint
hieroglyphics in the sand. I missed
the beach grass and beach plum,
the fatted seagull whose undazzled
eye stares down the sun; the distant
twirling weathercock, pivoting

sentry above my house whose watch
was never done.

"All right now, come about and head
back to shore." His voice came from
far away, far behind my carving prow,
my coracle, my Beetle Cat.
I bent a sturdier hand to secure
again the latches, a chronometer
formed inside my head ringing
out the watches. Too late now to step aside
and let my youth come back.

LORNA KNOWLES BLAKE

On Quivett Creek

We were not quite lost that Sunday
morning: two hours of high tide left

as the water began its alchemy from salt
to mineral, luring us into bosky silence—

small choirs in the pine trees, a breeze
ruffling the cordgrass, waves slapping

against the shore. Each turn compelled us
farther, we let ourselves go with the water,

forward; without charts, the looping ribbon
of creek became both route and destination.

Houses tucked into the marsh drowsed
behind drawn shades, indifferent to us,

shorebirds ignored us, busy with their own
tasks and hungers, and past the last bend,

or the next-to-last, past the osprey nesting
station, just before the cemetery, bells rang.

And if you were to die today, or leave me,
if memory is all we ever have of eternity,

this is the moment I'd choose to remember—
a green hereafter of sunlight and pealing bells.

Paddles raised, kayaks slowly pirouetting
in the sun, we floated, listening long after

the last echo's faint splash, until the tide
carried us on its backward journey to the bay.

SEAN KECK

Sea View Playland

Dennis Port, Massachusetts

At night, after dinner, the late pilgrims would come:
stretched out in a syncopated parade, children
with borrowed flashlights braving dark and skunks.

Still rimed with salt from a day in the waves,
they slapped in flip flops or tiptoed in bare feet,
brought part of the beach into The Barn of Fun.

Inside, the walls were painted green but danced
in particolored lights from whirring machines
that cast improvised stained glass over everything:

pinball games with flashes and bell rings, ten skee balls
thundering up ten ramps simultaneously, open-mouthed
Big Bertha yelling "Feed me! Feed me!"

Never enough quarters to satisfy that need.
The love tester and gypsy fortuneteller made futures
seem like something you could palm and read.

DIANE HANNA

Roaming Around the Brewster General Store

Who doesn't need three colors
of Emergency Beards tucked
in a side pocket, along with a bottle
of pirates' gold for days of identity crisis,
bone-thin want, crushing boredom.

Who doesn't want dark chocolate
Nonpareils melting on the tongue (or Necco
wafers or Sugar Babies) when summer
ebbs, and all sweet loves go home, leaving
shades pulled, cottages turned inward.

Who doesn't need nerd glasses,
dryer balls, embroidery floss, sunhats,
fly swatters, butterfly nets, buttons,
pink tutus, wind-up teeth, bicycle bells,
tomato soup, lamp chimneys, a muffin tin.

Who doesn't go a little wild in an old church
turned emporium, want to awaken the child
who tripped over wonder on the walk to school,
bent under a backpack heavy with someone else's
dreams. The child we forgot we lost.

TERRY S. JOHNSON

Brewster Cemetery

Sea Captains' Graveyard

Adeline, Allithena,
Lucy, Mercy, Polly,
lived day to day
with the wash
and the worry
weary with hope,
their men sailing
to far off places.
Maracaybo, Manzanilla.

Female society
well practiced
in funereal rites,
one Priscilla widowed
seventy-one years.

Barnabas, Freeman,
Joshua, Samuel, Seth,
lost at sea.
As they gulped the salt,
heaven swallowed.
Meet me there,
Meet me there.

BARBARA CROOKER

Eating Meltaways in Harwich Port

Bonatt's Bakery in Harwich Port

It's been four years since my father died,
and it seems like I'm becoming him,
driving my mother to this sandy spit
where we vacation with their friends
of thirty years, go to thrift shops
and lobster roll lunches at the white
Congregational church, admire the blue
hydrangeas bobbing along the picket fence.
This year, death's been busy as a surfcaster
on a moon-filled night, blues and stripers
running wild, reeling them in one after another:
Dottie talking on the phone, Merrick dozing
in his recliner, cancer's heavy weather
taking Jean and Clare, and only Mom and I remain.

We're sitting at our favorite restaurant, stirring
sugar in iced tea, hearing the little cubes tinkle
like wind chimes. I want to skip the next chapter,
stay here like this, life rolling on predictable
as morning fog or thick milky chowder, the sun,
a pat of butter, melting through. Our waitress,
in a white apron and pink uniform, her name scrolled
on her left breast, waits with a pad of paper:
"The meltaways just came out of the oven," she says.
"Can you smell them? I can put them in a box
if you don't have room for now."

ROBIN SMITH–JOHNSON

Bird Carver

Antique duck and goose decoys were sold ... for a record-setting $1.13 million each. ... The decoys were made by renowned carver A. Elmer Crowell of East Harwich, Mass.
          —Antiques and the Arts Weekly, Sept. 2007

He held his chisel just so, the same way
he held a 12-gauge as a boy.

From hunter to bird carver—
the shorebirds drawn to his decoys,

beauties made of cedar with pine heads.
His workshop a haven of precision:

Canada geese with sinuous necks
the gloss of dark bogs.

Pintail drakes, their long gray feathers
the sheen of open wetlands.

Red-breasted mergansers, each long bill
the shade of a marsh sunset.

Hundreds of birds that he sold here and there
or traded for a bucket of quahogs.

LINDA HAVILAND CONTE

Chatham's Seals at South Beach

Every fifteen minutes or so
a gang of them—seven or eight
together—patrols our chosen spot
at the beach. From the safety
of the waves, each Atlantic Gray
trains two round dark nostrils
and matching soulful eyes on
us, and lingers to make out
whether we are one of them.

They have little of the
timidity of forest creatures.
We expect they'll shimmy up
to introduce themselves shortly,
announcing the connection we've
forgotten. But, without warning, they
slip down the beach to their next
patrol point from the water.

They'll haul out on a private beach, officiously
laying claim to prime napping property,
blubbery back to bosom, forming with kin
a great oily raft of wriggle and snort.

LINDA HAVILAND CONTE

Harding's Beach

We'll go to the Cape today
and walk again to the lighthouse.
Almost nothing's there
but the trail and sky and glimpses of the sea.

Parts of the trail are rough and pebbly
and parts let your feet sink into
drifts like powdery snow.
Hardy scrub may be blooming
along the way: Dusty Miller, Rose Hips,
and purple Vetch.

Some grand cottages on the rise beyond the creek
will stare at us in their leisure as
we work out our worries on the trail.
We'll make it all the way to the lighthouse where
Chatham Roads channel meets Stage Harbor
and watch the sailboats and fishing vessels
come and go. We'll return by the breezier
Nantucket Sound if it's sunny and getting hot.

We'll come home feeling well-used
and in possession of a plan
even if it's only dinner in town.
We've sloughed off the old skin of our feet
so many times on that trail, it will know us
when we return.

JUDITH ASKEW

Orleans Parade, July 4

[An excerpt]

My cousins put this family Fourth of July
celebration together so coherently:
People who bear little gifts arrive on time;
we park, then find our prearranged chairs

along the parade route; the children
don't cry or fall down. The Grand
Marshall appears, followed by the ramrod
veterans stepping lively step-in-step.

And now here comes a band, so many grey heads
tromboning and trumpeting; then huge shiny red or yellow
fire engines, magnificent works of contemporary art,
all chrome and splendor; bagpipes that send

goosebumps along my arms. *Look*, I say
to my cousin, showing her how much I love bagpipes.
Have them at your funeral, she says. *Put it in your will*.
I'm so caught up in good feelings

that even the thought of my death brings
a smile at this idea dropped so nonchalantly
into the tangle of flying candies, children on bicycles,
women on the Willy's Gym float hefting

Styrofoam barbells, and dogs from the vet hospital
spaced just so, wearing their red silk lobster costumes.

MAXINE SUSMAN

Henry Beston's Outermost House, 1927

> Eastham, Cape Cod

He builds his dune shack on the bluff
above the marsh, the edge a few feet off
with views of open sea,

walks the beach all weather, seasons,
all times of day and night, miles to town,
carrying food home in a rucksack across Nauset.

After driving an ambulance in France, Verdun,
the ocean's onslaughts, the pounding storms
and battery of gales hit pure—

not like waves of dead and dying men.
Shipwrecks on the Outer Cape claim
mere dozens at a time. A year living alone,

witnessing, then returning to his shack
to hone sentences like calligraphy
chiselled on sand when tide flows out,

a whole chapter turned over to nothing
but ocean sounds for pages and pages,
various as the flight patterns of birds.

SHARON TRACEY

The Outermost House

Here is the humble house
Henry Beston built in '25
and came to
in solitude
a humble house with windows
on all sides
to be with the birds,
the fish, the pinpoint stars.

Set in the dunes
and later left
to fight the wind,
the encroaching sands.

A lonely-looking humble house.

In '76, we visit the house in daylight
then wait for night, a chance
to drag our sleeping
bags between two crests of dune
nestled near the house.

Crawl in, the light a crescent moon.

Listen as the waves slurp
a messy line between two worlds.

Who knew the blizzard of '78
would come

in two short years
to take the humble house away.

Like anyone or any house,
what is lived will wash away.

MATTHEW THORBURN

Three Sisters

—for Lillian

Not Chekhov's, but Nauset's
three wooden lighthouses,
moved inland in 1911 and out
of service, so they wouldn't
topple over with the eroding
coastal shelf and wind up
in the water, now are found
here in a field—this pocket
of yellow grass tucked away
in the woods—so we can only
imagine their lights, which
have long since been turned off,
sweeping across the leaves
that wave in the trees to warn
the ships, which are not there,
not to drift in too close
to the rocks, which are not here.

JOSEPH STANTON

Edward Hopper's Color Notes for Route 6, Eastham

After Hopper designed a scene,
he'd plan his colors.

His notes for this picture place
"pale green" on one wall,
"pale warm grey" on another,
"pale lavender" on still another.

His shadows tumble in one direction
as "dark warm lavender,"
and as "cold shadow" in the other.
All he wanted, he once said,
was to paint sunlight
on the side of a building.

Here we see him flicking on
Cape Cod light
one color at a time.

GAIL MAZUR

Eastham Turnips, November

Honor System, the sign tacked to a scrub oak said,
and on the table a rusty tin box with a slot in the lid

next to a pile of dirty purplish-white turnips beside
a battered trembly scale. Eastham turnips Eastham

was once "famous" for, fall staple from the rocky ground
hapless settlers had no choice but to farm centuries ago,

back when there were forests, before the black walnut
trees were felled to build Cape houses and whaling boats.

The last of the turnip farm stands alongside a highway
that never existed when Eastham was all farms. What

else could grow here in the hardscrabble soil? Today, no
sign or scale, just an empty table, a dead patch of grass.

Trusted by strangers I'd never seen, I liked folding soft
George Washingtons through the slot for history's sake

and bringing root vegetables home, and finding recipes
to make the bitter delicious. Gratins. Frittatas. Soups.

JAMES W. KERSHNER

Fort Hill

At dawn on New Year's Day
we gather in resolution
atop the easternmost promontory
of Cape Cod's "bared and bended arm."

Fort Hill—a bulwark
against backsliding.

Intricate salt marshes teem below,
barrier beach beyond,
then crashing breakers,
and miles of roiling sea.

Sometimes it seems
we can almost see Portugal.

MARGE PIERCY

Money Moves In

When I moved here the road called Cobb
Farm actually led to a farm, where
in fall we'd clean out the chicken house
for free to feed our vegetables.

You could buy eggs still warm from
a hen's body. On a rolling meadow
in Eastham, a family raised and sold
ducks. The Old King's Highway led

for miles, a sandy track through forest
without a house, now subdivisions. I
dug arrowheads where houses crouch
on lawns empty ten months a year.

The ocean beach was a shell picker's
paradise where now tampon covers,
oil clots and plastic bottles wash up.
Foxes lived on the hill long flattened.

No Trespassing signs are common
as tree frogs used to be. Rich folks
claim the beaches and exile oyster
farmers, families without trust funds.

We may be the last generation to think
butterflies are common. Where did all
the box turtles go? This land I love
I have watched turn into real estate.

80

I have seen it vanish under huge houses
nobody needs, decks wide enough to land
helicopters on with views of others with too
much money they waste, creating waste.

MARY BERGMAN

Disappearing (Coast Guard Beach)

There is no resisting the ocean.
Assures the narrator's measured voice
in the new Park Service film.

The Outermost House
flashes across the screen, swirling in waves.
The park ranger utters a quiet *no, no.*

Humans will adapt.
Music swells and the camera pulls back,
revealing our narrow ribbon of sand.

And how can every beautiful and painful thing
that seems to have ever happened to me
be contained in this shifting place?

A lot of people cry at that part, the ranger nods.

In the late afternoon light of winter
reeds around the salt pond glow golden.
The water looks inviting. How easy it would be
to slip away with the tide. To disappear.

BRENDAN GALVIN

An Unsigned Postcard from Wellfleet

This face evolved out of the bay's conditions
as surely as boats take shape over time
from the waters they work. On a picture postcard
now, the horizon behind him nearly flatlining,

oyster bucket and rake by his hipboots,
soft hat at a tilt, almost western, it's Veenie
the clam warden, king of the flats,
hands on hips the only sign of his authority.

Was I seven last time I saw him, brought
by my older cousins to see his cows
and chickens, and relay some message
from his ancient friend our grandpa,

who lived only five minutes across
the old state road? Iconic now, a word
I'll bet he'd hate, on this postcard
he's "The Wellfleet Oysterman."

Who sent this test of memory? Almost
seventy years I've carried this face with me
through schools and jobs and the common streets,
but never saw another quite like it.

Behind the camera he's winking or squinting at,
I can even remember there'd be
a field of goldenrod this time of year.

ALEXIS IVY

Booth #51 at the Wellfleet Flea Market

A woman sells sea glass and costume
jewelry. Sea glass should be found, not bought.
I almost want to tell her that.
I have a bucketful of sea glass
I've already picked up on the beach this summer.
I know tide charts.
The tide is high this afternoon.
I pick up sea glass—so many the same
when I walk the same bay each day,

each summer. I first pick up all of them.
I make a pile on the beach where
I compare which ones are more
interesting, which have more detail,
toss the ones with seaweed guck stuck,
or barnacles. Blues are the rarest.
Choosing what I want for keeps.
The ones wet enough to shine. Glisten.

I should ask her if those are her findings
of the sea. Her collection she's
gotten tired of keeping.

GAIL MAZUR

Shipwreck

—Winter, Wellfleet, 2008

Sweet carcass of an ark, the past's oaken belly—
what the sands had buried a storm uncovered
high on Newcomb Hollow beach; a hull,

round wooden pegs, tool marks that tell
its serious age, ribs like the bony cage
of a Great White whale, washed up

on the shoals a decade after the Civil War, a schooner,
archaeologists say, converted to a barge—
they think she carried coal up the Atlantic coast

from an impoverished post-War South,
coal that washed ashore on the outer Cape
to the hardscrabble townspeople's shivering relief.

In a few weeks, they're sure the tides will resettle her,
she'll be washed back out to sea or she'll merge again,
fill with the coarse sands shifting beneath your feet.

Homely, heavy, sea-scoured, why should she seem
a venerable thing, spiritual, why should you long
to touch her, to stretch out under the March sun

in the long smooth silvery frame of a cradle
or curl like an orphaned animal on the hand-cut planks
and caress the marks, the trunnels, with your mittened paws?

Is it that she hints much yet tells little of the souls lost
with her, the mystery of survival, the depths she's traveled?
Has she heard the music on the ocean floor, instrumentation

of Mantis Shrimp, the *bong bong* of Humming Fish?
Why does the day, all blues and greys, feel transcendental?
She's a remnant, a being almost completely effaced, yet to you

still resonant—can anything this gone be consecrated? Experts
have examined the braille of her hull, weighed the evidence
and they declare, *It's another secret the ocean burped up*,

nothing but a blip, a brief reappearance, once rowdy,
rough with purpose, now not even a container, holding
nothing, revealing nothing....But aren't you also a singular secret

Nature burped up, hurled flailing into the air from the start,
hungry for light, holding onto whatever buoys you,
alive, kicking, even when you know you're going down?

STEVEN BAUER

Marconi Station: South Wellfleet

From this height and in this calm
we can see almost to Europe, and the waves
curl toward us like open parentheses, cupped fire
in their uncompleted curls. If ocean
is a word, like *month* or *year*, we use

to measure time, its slow erosion
of this cliff took longer
than the average life. Marconi built
four towers to send his invisible words,
and what remains crumbles back to sand.

All the ways I had of trying to talk.
I set fires on the dark plain, smoke
ascended in a vacuum the sky built. Tongue
twisted with dashes and dots, arms
like semaphores. Some days I was a ship

in distress, the wireless stuttered
mayday and the ocean drowned the call.
This need to speak out of myself
does nothing for the sun's dazzle
and spark, a rawness the season breeds.

North toward Truro, two boats
trawl the quiet water. Whatever we think
the wind steals away from us. But the waves
flash back, electromagnetic, a measured silence
where words aren't necessary, and the heart goes on.

PAULA ERICKSON

Hamblen Farm Morning, Wellfleet

Overalls over thermals
all tucked into rubber boots
coffeed and fed enough to go on
buckets, rake and Elke in the truck,
we hiccup the dirt road to the farm.

A February thaw gives rise
to whiffs of feverfew and the old cedar,
its fruit scattered juniper blue
against pale grass,
the mudded earth forgiving
and soft underfoot.

Mind easing, I set to work
casting aged manure,
darning dark furrows,
tucking garlic under
a mantle of cord grass
winnowed by the sea.

My dog finishes her survey
of invisible wild things,
sees I am too dull to play,
settles with a sigh
atop her new mulch bed.

When hunger calls
for a second breakfast
I gather tools and load up.

Something—a stick perhaps,
rings the tailpipe like a bell
as if to consecrate the morning.

ALAN FELDMAN

I Come Back from a Sail

It's December, and no one would want to sail
up here in New England—no one, that is, who's sane—
though sanity's not a requirement for sailors. The sea
doesn't care, sloshing or raging against the same shore
as in summer, but the fierce wind, cold as steel,
makes most of us huddle beside a fire on land.

Sometimes I wonder what it would be like to land
on Jeremy Point at a time like this—not a sail
on the razor edge of the horizon, or on the blue steel
of the bay. What does it matter, staying sane,
when my thoughts drift away from words towards the shore
of dreams, or captionless pictures, my ears ringing with the sea

wind that makes the island's grasses wild. Only at sea
does the brain become what confronts it, the waves that land
on the foredeck, the sheets in my hand. It shores
me up, when I'm scattered. I come back from a sail,
feel nothing's complicated, and that I'm sane
even if the world's not. It's as if sleep's been stealing

over me. Or not sleep. My bones turning to steel
so I can't be rattled. I suppose I love the sea,
though I fear it. Or because I do. It's sane
to get scared by the force of it, unimaginable on land,
the cruelty of the gale snapping the loose sail
like a whip. And the hopeless distance to the shore

that must be crossed to get out of its grip. On shore

90

it's difficult to guess how vast, pitiless, and steely
those forces can be. But try going out under sail
and double-reefed. I've seen the sea
milk-white, the air so full of sleet the land's
another universe. I suppose it's insane

to be out there. But I guess it's sane
to know what we're up against. If you stay on shore
you have to strain to listen, the gods on land
not often speaking above a whisper. But off-shore
in the cold, steel claws of terror, they roar.

BRENDAN GALVIN

An Intermission

After the last snows and the first
April chive-bursts, two came in
off the flyway, not flying
but coasting, humped to catch the air,
their wings on the long glide
without a single beat. White as if
a breeze were buffing fresh snowbanks,
their wing-sound was like wind
over snow—two tundra swans
by their black bills, not the decorative
imports children toss old bread at
on public water, but long as a man
and spanned wide as an eagle. It was
as though some epic I read forty years ago
had drawn them out of my mind
into the air. *Cygnus columbianus,*
named for the river Lewis and Clark
found them on, they had come
all the way from Currituck Sound
or the Chesapeake to the Little Pamet, aimed for
the high Arctic nesting grounds. Like gods
out of their element, they floated past me
above the pond and on down
the riverine marshes, pagan, twinned,
impersonal in their cold sublimity,
blind to my witness, their necks
outsnaking, intent on a brief rest
somewhere on our little river.

LUCILE BURT

Kayaking the Upper Pamet in May

Come along and float
just inches above the muck,
dense with death and life,
on water still frigid from snow melt
and days on end of April rain
that reached cold into our bones.

Come along and thaw
in air thick with the chorus
of bayberry blossom, first leaves
of swamp maple, birch, scrub oak,
of fiddleheads unfurling,
of red-winged blackbird, yellow warbler.

Thick too with old longings
rising in our chests
like the ancient snapping turtle
stained with river tannin
fringed with algae,
surfacing for another spring.

KEITH ALTHAUS

Late Bus, Provincetown

What did we want
from our lives?

Someone has taken
the question-mark
and hammered it
back into a stick,
just as they have
straightened the roads
whose very turning
is their beauty.

Recently on the side
of a building
on the town wharf
a local photographer has installed
four large black & white panels,
close-ups of old Portuguese women,
fishermen's wives.
They look out
all day, all night,
on the harbor, listen
to the Town Hall bell
after the last bus has arrived
and departed and the last couple
has passed under or around
the lampposts' cones of light.

The faces are meant

to stir within us
both a sense of the tragic
frailty and the harshness
of life, made bearable
only by the beauty
of courage and sacrifice.
Unlike the granite monument
on top of the hill which feels
the wind and rain and snow
intermittently, these faces
are exposed every day
to the spray of the surf
and are soaked
by the tides below.
Already they've been
taken down twice
for repair and restoration.
Yet their eyes never blink
or close like a doll's
laid on its back.
They do not look, but stare
at everything: the breakwater,
floats, gulls, the fleet
coming in, trailing clouds
of bird-life, raucous,
joyful as a sudden
whirlwind of litter
on a corner in the city.

KEITH ALTHAUS

From the Pilgrim Monument

for Roger Skillings

The climb is breathtaking,
the view roughly medieval:
on one side, the town's
boat-filled harbor
and traffic-clogged streets;
on the other, graveyards,
mute and still, stretching to the edge
of the moon-like dunes,
forever changing, shifting,
being taken away (the tallest one
already halved since we arrived here
thirty years ago), and nothing
added or put back except
beach grass planted to slow
the process, and a little dust,
ashes of friends who loved it here,
and wanted to stay, or go
wherever it is going.

FRED MARCHANT

Pilgrim Spring

it's not where you think
it is it's not even where

the map says it should be
though you've been here

many times before you still
don't know where it is you

walk down gravel winter
paths and listen to a scrub

oak talking dead talk with
frozen leaves and seagrass

the icy winter dunes and
an end of days sky while

a small hiding creature stirs
as you pass and you think

it just might guide you to
the place where you can

kneel and sip trying to take
in what the spring offers

broken arms and lost lives
reaching up from under

the frozen ground you walk
and the history hidden in

the sweet water welling up
somewhere around here out

on the farthest edge of who
we as a nation and people are

ROSALIND PACE

Province Lands Dunes

Here I learn how not to make a difference,
for the dunes change by the hour, the sea
comes in, goes out, in front of me, in back
of me, the horizon is all around, everything
is on the edge. This shack leans into the sand.
Fingers of pitch pine roots touch its grey step.

For these few days, I am living here.
I love all this unconditionally because I can
keep none of it. What keeps such longing
for the forever rising and falling

as each wave breaks itself on the shore?
Single grasses in the night are blown
like compasses and at dawn stand up
in the center of their delicate perfect circles.

EGAN MILLARD

Promised Land

the moment I first saw the Province Lands
        prophecy snapping into perigee
on Route 6, from the hill at Pilgrim Heights
        restless, queer and twenty
it seemed somehow familiar and foreknown
        the lake and the harbor—two bowls of sky
the cottages that line the strip of beach
        the dunes that wander naked and wild
like waves that rolled ashore and turned to gold

this was the Zion I'd had visions of
        my young nerves burning, mind swarming
searching for reasons to remain alive
        staring down fake ferns in doctors' offices, mumbling
a hope to live for—harbor for the soul
        not a grain of shame on faces in the streets
where men can let themselves be loved
        where kindred spirits spark with heat
where one world ends, another one begins

HOWARD FAERSTEIN

Provincetown

There were mulberry limbs twined with mimosa branches leaning close to the back door. Stretching, I could barely reach the fruit hanging high above a narrow path. Mulberries for breakfast, mulberries with lunch, our teeth stained that whole week. Each of us believed the other was dreaming. Imagination wasn't necessary. Late afternoons we took the small, crooked side streets leading to the harbor, passing scrolled awnings and furled flags, porches intaglioed by purple morning glories. A raft of eider ducks with their black bellies and white backs visible from the bleached wharf. It was July 4th, nearing dusk, when we joined the promenade up Commercial Street. Couples arm-in-arm: men with men, women with women, women with men. The smell of mud at low tide. A street musician played a Bach suite on her viola, an elegantly dressed woman sang from *Carmen* in faulty French. Down one clamshell alleyway, I thought I heard a bobwhite's whistled call, perhaps answering those first explosions. Long Point Light and Pilgrim Monument always in the distance, the mast of the schooner, *Rose Dorothea*, threatening to rise through the library steeple. And at every open space between crowded shops, at every corner, fireworks erupting. The children's moon at first quarter as the sun dropped lower. Already the days beginning to shorten. Once we reached the West End breakwater, we forgot everything. That's what we told each other. Imagination wasn't necessary. Each of us believing the other was dreaming. Then we swung round and strolled back, stopping in a painter's studio where a show was being hung. The artist said, *I don't want to know what I'm painting.* But every move she'd made had intention, every step we took, the bleeding berries, bobwhite calling its mate, light tumbling off ringed constellations, each star in the ladder tipping over, spilling song, filling the darkness that finally stretches over land's end, the bursting flame over half the world.

SUSAN JO RUSSELL

Membrane

Macmillan Pier, Provincetown

The cormorant dives
under the boardwalk where boys four abreast
take up its breadth jostle and slouch
jeans dropped to the ass skin itchy
ready to molt
they're helpless to grasp
what they're breaking out of
into

while four girls
tasteful bikinis streaming hair
poise on the edge of the pier on a dare they rise
haughty and sleek on their toes bare
backs to the water
as if on a signal arcs of four bodies
pierce the air and everything
stops—

boys old ladies toddlers mothers
cries of the gulls boats in the harbor
wind-strewn moon pale in its orbit caught
at the moment of flight—
and everyone's flying
and everyone's sinking
into the quiet into the danger
until

splashes laughter
four heads bobbing like seals in the harbor
and it all cranks up
the afternoon warms the moon climbs higher
boys shamble on punching shoulders
old ladies stroll to the end of the boardwalk
where the cormorant
rises

LUCILE BURT

Surfcasting

Solitary men in waders
line the shore at first light.
The sea is a dappled purple.
They are watching for signs:
the churn of baitfish,
the cacophonous swirl of gulls.
They are thinking of fish,
not women.

They cast with the whole arc of body.
The weighted line carries
the barbed question mark
out into deep water.
No one wants the easy answers:
flat rippling wings of skate,
tangle of rubbery sea ribbon,
even the bluefish, so voracious
it will strike anything.

The men wait with the patience of herons,
or the restless circling of terns.
They are willing to go away empty
unless they can land the splendid,
wily prize, the striped bass
whose hard strike bows the rod,
whose fight arcs it high out of the water,
where it dances for a moment on air,
a gray and silver shimmer,
a leap of shining muscle.

104

These are not grizzled fishermen
chugging out at night in trawlers
to Stellwagen Bank, where in deep water
their nets will gather so many fish
that none surprises. This is sport,
not livelihood, a story
about luck and the right lure,
rod bent at the strike, the fight.

Once the fish is landed,
they are indifferent.
They can send it back, take it home,
either way.

CAROL MALAQUIAS

Memoirs of a Fisherman's Son

The artists' kids' crayons were worn down to stumps.
The fishermen's kids,
all we knew how to draw were boats,
with a pencil.

Provincetown in the fifties and sixties
was homey and provincial.
The New York arts scene
gave my boyhood innocence
a little sophistication.

My father Charlie Max, born *Carlos*,
came through Ellis Island, a baby.
He made a fair living on his dragger *Revenge*

Yet never as much money
as Cap'n Charlie's Seafood,
where my mother sold her clam chowder
and kale soup
to Julie Newmar
and Abe Burrows.

Rumor had it
Elvis Presley was in town
but he didn't even like fish.

We called ourselves Portagees.
Nicknames happened to everyone.
Duna, Dory Plug, Ducky.

106

Jazz Garters, Joe Bucket, Joe Fat.
Charlie Max looked only
a little like a Mexican.
Mex became Max.

My sister had a crush on Tommy Thomas
who looked like Elvis.
He had a beautiful skiff
with an engine, a gift from his *vovo*.
I was so envious.
A boat was better than a car.

Every boy had to have a boat.
Each spring, I'd meticulously paint
my homemade pram
the *Little Max*.

The starving artists
would hang around the wharf
hoping for a handout.
Henry Hensche would arrive
on his bicycle.
"Hey, Charlie, you got any fish?"
My father would toss one up to him.
I wish we had one of his paintings in return.
To Charlie Max,
payback wasn't a consideration
for someone in need.

ALICE KOCIEMBA

Homage to the Patricia Marie

after the painting by Salvatore Del Deo

All seven crew missing, all presumed
dead. The boy, in blue, stares wide-eyed,
away from the headline, his dead mother's name.
Come home smelling like money, she'd have said.

Dead. The captain, Billy, found blue and wide-eyed,
clinging to a buoy, three miles off Nauset.
Come home smelling like money, she'd have said,
dreaming of scallops piled high in the hold.

Still clinging, that's Billy—son and grandson of captains,
his boat named after his young, first wife.
This trip, the scallops filled the hold like a dream,
before a *freaker* swept them all into the deep,

along with the boat—a second death for his wife.
We choose the life and the life chooses us.
That *freaker* took their dragger into the deep,
leaving only debris and the crew to wash up.

They chose the life and the life took theirs.
Dicky and Buddy never were found.
Just debris and five bodies came home that winter:
Billy, Bobby, Walter, Ernest, Mott.

Dicky and Buddy forever lost
in Pollack's Rip, where the sea gets real sloppy.

108

Billy, Bobby, Walter, Mott. . .
I think we found your husband. This key fits your lock.

In Pollack's Rip, the sea gets real sloppy.
On the wharf, a fisherman reads from the paper.
They only knew it was Ernest when his key fit her lock.
The men listen, hand to shoulder, shells an empty blue.

The fisherman reads on, the paper now shaking.
All seven crew missing, all presumed dead.
The men listen, hand to shoulder, as empty blue eyes
look away from the headline, his dead mother's name.

BRENDAN GALVIN

Kale Soup

The Mayflower Café, the Vets' Club on
Shankpainter Road, or maybe Cookie's Tap
before the name and linoleum
vanished and pork chops *vinha d'alhos,*
meaning "wine of garlic,"
and *ameijoas,* meaning littleneck quahogs,
got kicked off the menu. Or maybe
you tried it first from a
back-of-the-stove stockpot in some
grandmother's kitchen, a dark,
fertile root of a woman
who drove to the hill above
Race Point and sat till she sighted
the family boat hauling home
from Georges Bank. In all those places
it was the same and different, with
or without carrots, with or without
chicken or lamb left over
from Sunday, but always simmered a day
over heat so low it never
raised a bubble, and built
with plenty of this, a little
of that, some more of the other,
a text brought by heart
from the Azores, when names like
Codhina and Gaspar entered
the whalers' logbooks. Always
linguica in it, which put the oak
in the forearms of dorymen,

110

vinegar for the vinegar of it,
chourico for setting the otter trawls,
garlic and cumin that thickened
the blood and sent trapboats
toward sunrise and the bluefins
thrashing and cruising
in a jerry-rig of nets and stakes.
You bought a store downtown
and painted it heliotrope
to catch summer people. You called it
garbage soup and denied you ever
ate it. But some nights in autumn,
coming home, you pass through a fog
so husky with smoked pork and spices
you're gaffed by the hook
of this whole peninsula.

M. BROCKETT–DEVINE

Blue Skies

Rainy morning in Provincetown.
Blue Skies—a trawler fresh
from an early haul—pulls inside
the piled-rock breakwater. Her blue hull—
darker than a robin's egg, lighter
than the blue field of her American flag—
is rust stained, worn from days
of rubbing tide-after-tide against the rubber-
padded pilings of the concrete dock.

In Niantic, Connecticut,
no captain paints his hull blue.
There, the color is bad luck—an insult
to the sea. To mimic the ocean's blue skin
is to mock her, to tempt Poseidon—a jealous god,
an angry god—to rise through the waves,
clasp a boat in his crusher-claw grip,
and fracture her hull before
anyone can loosen a life raft.

But here, at the tip of the Cape, the color
is sacred. It honors the heavens and asks
the Holy Infant to keep them afloat and their nets full.
The crew ties the boat to her berth, waits
for the icehouse to open, for the packing crew
to arrive. They smoke. Some talk
in Portuguese. Others in English. All wonder
what price the market will offer for two dozen
totes of gray sole—all that was caught

in these days of closed fisheries,
weekly quotas, and the decimation
of nearly every known and edible species.

Consider the tilefish: unknown until 1879
when fishermen found them feeding
on the Continental Shelf, where the warm Gulf Stream
heats the water off the coast. Imagine
their surprise when that first sweet-meated
fish, some say tastes like lobster, others like crab,
rose on their hook—its skin blue (darker than
a robin's egg, lighter than the blue field of the American
flag), its yellow spots flickering like cold flames,
and its wet scales refracting the sun into tiny rainbows.
Imagine their puzzled looks when months later
the sea was awash in dead fish, a quick dip of arctic
waters freezing the tilefish feeding grounds,
gray fish bouncing off the bows of their boats
as they cut through the rotting flotilla.

Ten years passed before another live tile
was found. Come 1970, the fleet,
hungry for new game, was ready to try
that fishery once more.

Still raining.
The crew of the *Silver Mink* arrives
to do some up-keep. They met their quota
for the week, won't fish again until Friday.
They'll grease the winch, change a water pump,
adjust the "doors" that keep the net dragging the bottom,
its mouth open, ready to swallow fish. The first mate calls out
to the *Blue Skies'* captain. He shrugs in reply.

I've seen that shrug.

My father, away for a week at a time,
was out for tile in the 70's. At first,
he'd say 40,000 pounds in one week. 30,000 pounds
another. The white hull of his boat stained brown
from washing blood off the decks each night.
Longlining: Every 6 feet another hook,
another tilefish. Their scales, like tiny bathroom tiles,
flaked onto my father's pants, onto his boots, into
his hair, into his laundry so that days after he left for sea
my brother and I would find the milky-gray scales
on the couch, in the car, in our rooms.
20,000, 12,000, 10,000 pounds in two weeks
and the boat would pull in and my father
would just look at us—and shrug.

Now, in Niantic, he sells tickets to tourists
and takes them out to grounds where there used
to be cod. Used to be flounder. Used to be fluke,
bluefish, and bass. It's how he pays the bills.
But the crew who remember what fishing used to be
whistle the theme song from Gilligan's Island
as they cast off the lines and show people
how to use a reel, how to bait a hook. "We didn't promise
to catch you fish," they say when passengers complain
about their empty burlap sacks. "We promised
to take you fishing. Your line's in the water—you're fishing."

On the Cape, a packer raises the icehouse door.
He wears his yellow rain slickers,
their black straps crossed against his bare back.
He stands inside, smokes one more before his hands get slick
from the slime seeping out of the dead soles' skin.
He's just 25, too young to remember when packers worked
without stopping 10 or 12 hours a shift. When the icehouses
were open all day, every day, when the boat crews

complained of nets nearly snapped from the weight
of cod, or half-day hauls that left their boats
staggered in the bay, outriggers down like wings for balance,
while the crews cut fish into the night. Of the slick
of guts and blood that filled the harbor, the sky dark
with gulls mobbing the waves for every scrap.

The crew prepares to unload, wash down,
and lock down. No one mentions the old days:
Those who were there can't bear to remember;
those who weren't can't begin to imagine.

The packer squints against the rain
blowing in the door. The gray morning
will offer little diversion. He stares
at a spot on the pier where yesterday,
in the sun, three boys jumped
at low tide, dropping 15 feet before splashing
into the blue-green water. They laughed and yelled
"Get out of the way!" as they leaped in
one after the other. It was something to watch.
Something to pass the time between boats.

ELIZABETH BRADFIELD

Historic Numbers of Right Whales Skim Feeding off Cape Cod

Who would expect their appetite
would come to seem ominous?
But now I know

they are voids of hunger. They plough
a field of plankton, turn,
plough again. They strip the water

like loggers on a clearcut.
The bay this spring seemed overrun
by stern, enormous beetles:

black, vaguely military, inexorable.

Poor plankton, adrift
in flailing clouds, poor blushing copepods
with delicate antennae, watermelon scent—

you don't stand a chance.
Week after week, right whales
eat the bay down

until they have to leave it.
Time and proximity have made them
monsters. This must be how it was before.

ELIZABETH BRADFIELD

Concerning the Proper Term for a Whale Exhaling

Poof my mother sighs
as against the clearcut banks near Hoonah
another humpback exhales, its breath
white and backlit by sun.
                                Don't
say that, says my father, disapproving
of such casual terminology or uneasy
with the tinge of pink tulle, the flounce
poof attaches to the thing we're watching, beast
of hunt, of epic migrations.
                                        But I'm the naturalist,
suggesting course and speed for approach. They
are novices, and the word is mine,
brought here from the captains I sailed for
and the glittering Cape Cod town
where we docked each night
after a day of watching whales.
                                Poof,
Todd or Lumby would gutter,
turning the helm, my cue to pick up
the microphone. Coming from those smoke-roughed cynics
who call the whales dumps, rank the tank-topped talent
on the bow, and say each time they set a breaching calf
in line with the setting sun, *What do you think of that? Now that's
what I call pretty*, then sit back,
light a cigarette—coming from them,
I loved the word.
                                And even more
because the dock we returned to each night

teemed with summer crowds, men lifting
their hands to other men, the town
flooded with poufs free to flutter, to cry, as they can't
in Newark or Pittsburgh or Macon, to let
their love rise into the clear, warm air,
to linger and glow
for a brief time visible.

MARK DOTY

Atlantis: Michael's Dream

Michael writes to tell me his dream:
I was helping Randy out of bed,
supporting him on one side
with another friend on the other,

and as we stood him up, he stepped out
of the body I was holding and became
a shining body, brilliant light
held in the form I first knew him in.

This is what I imagine will happen,
the spirit's release. Michael,
when we support our friends,
one of us on either side, our arms

under the man or woman's arms,
what is it we're holding? Vessel,
shadow, hurrying light? All those years
I made love to a man without thinking

how little his body had to do with me;
now, diminished, he's never been so plainly
himself—remote and unguarded,
an otherness I can't know

the first thing about. I said,
You need to drink more water
or you're going to turn into
an old dry leaf. And he said,

Maybe I want to be an old leaf.
In the dream Randy's leaping into
the future, and still here, Michael's holding him
and releasing at once. Just as Steve's

holding Jerry, though he's already gone,
Marie holding John, gone, Maggie holding
her John, gone, Carlos and Darren
holding another Michael, gone,

and I'm holding Wally, who's going.
Where isn't the question,
though we think it is;
we don't even know where the living are,

in this raddled and unraveling "here."
What is the body? Rain on a window,
a clear movement over whose gaze?
Husk, leaf, little boat of paper

and wood to mark the speed of the stream?
Randy and Jerry, Michael and Wally
and John: lucky we don't have to know
what something is in order to hold it.

CAROL A. AMATO

At Beech Forest

In memory of Mary Oliver

She walked here
often and early
before the day
escaped the clouds
entering the woods
on the boardwalk
where chickadees,
used to hand-feeding,
greet each passerby
by chittering and bouncing
from branch to branch.

Then she,
along the flattened dunes
that once may have risen
higher, traveled the gradually
ascending trail slowly
as always,
paying attention.

She followed
the gnarly roots
of ancient beeches
that dug under bright
green mosses
and may have known
the pain of those

whose smooth skin,
gouged with the initials
of impermanent souls,
still rose with dignity
far above
the taut flesh
of their trunks.

She was well acquainted
with the other trees;
oak (white and black),
maple, hemlock, pitch pine;
I don't know if she talked
to them but if she did,
they answered.
She saw in the swampy
shallows of Blackwater Pond
the cattails that burst
and scattered their fluffy
progeny across the pond
in the fall;
the fox sunning on a bank
in summer;
the turtle crossing the trail
to lay her eggs
in spring;
the black snake winding
through the short grass
thinking it can't be seen.

I walk here now.
Have you noticed? she asks me
and missing her,
I have.

CATHERINE R. CRYAN

Mary Oliver, Reading

August 2012, Fine Arts Work Center

She read what
she wrote of owls + swamps +
    black oaks, all
the things dear + vital
        in my marshy, overgrown heart.

Perfection, when it comes, is startling.
  Art invites what we
  never were expecting.

To stand in a doorway, watch
  + listen, be aware
  of what falls   into
        the mind's stillwater: words,
droplets off cherry twigs from
        a ceased rain, notes
  of thrush-song from a high railing.

CATHIE DESJARDINS

Stanley's Garden

for Stanley Kunitz 1905–2006

Keeping the ocean on my left,
I wended through Provincetown
the summer after he died,
past the landscape galleries,
roller skating drag queens,
the ice cream and T-shirt shops,
and hand-carried dogs
with apologetic eyes—

to a quieter part of town.
I didn't know if I could find
his house, but there
was the rusty gate.

Here were the good bones of the stone
terraces he'd built, hauling loads
of seaweed from the beach
half a century ago.

I'd imagined it as somber,
overgrown, since he'd died.
But the leaves and petals
shimmied in the sunlight,
his beloved wind anemones
swaying gently. All, all
was nearly vibrating with joy.

He'd caressed these plants,
just as, the one time
I met him and read him a poem,
he took my face gently
in his hands, a poet
a hundred years old
touching me as if
I were a flower.

MARK DOTY

Long Point Light

Long Point's apparitional
    this warm spring morning,
        the strand a blur of sandy light,

and the square white
    of the lighthouse—separated from us
        by the bay's ultramarine

as if it were nowhere
    we could ever go—gleams
        like a tower's ghost, hazing

into the rinsed blue of March,
    our last outpost in the huge
        indetermination of sea.

It seems cheerful enough,
    in the strengthening sunlight,
        fixed point accompanying our walk

along the shore. Sometimes I think
    it's the where-we-will be,
        only not yet, like some visible outcropping

of the afterlife. In the dark
    its deeper invitations emerge:
        green witness at night's end,

flickering margin of horizon,

marker of safety and limit.
      but limitless, the way it calls us,

and where it seems to want us
      to come. And so I invite it
         into the poem, to speak,

and the lighthouse says:
      Here is the world you asked for,
         gorgeous and opportune,

here is nine o'clock, harbor-wide,
      and a glinting code: promise and warning.
         The morning's the size of heaven.

What will you do with it?

DIANE LOCKWARD

The Properties of Light

> *Isn't the whole world heaven's coast?*
> —from *Heaven's Coast,* Mark Doty

I come for the light, the artist says.
Dawn and again at sunset,
he goes to the Provincetown beach,
sets up his easel. At just the right angle,
he can catch that light on the canvas.

He uses words like *shimmer, glow, radiance.*
He talks about what our forefathers must have seen
when they woke that first dawn just off the coast.
He darkens the room, lights up the wall
with his slides. We see
not the play of light against dark,
but the play of light against light.
We see it in the rocks, the beached whale,
the bones of dead fish.

In the last days of my father's life,
he kept calling *me—Elaine, Elaine—*
even though I was in the next room
or the same room and he didn't need
or want anything. He kept doing it.
If I answered, he'd know
he was still alive. If I didn't,
he was dead.

The last time he called, he held out

his hand, all blue veins and bones now.
His **head** fell back, and the skin
on his face smoothed out.

What I remember is the **light**,
how it slipped into the room and took him.
In that moment, the light was different,
and I saw my father as I had never seen
him before—young, full of wonder,
and in no pain at all.

JENNIFER MARKELL

Landscape with Painters

Provincetown, MA

Undeterred by record heat,
they've come to paint the marsh.
Donning straw hats
and baseball caps, the class spreads out
with aprons, crimped tubes of oils,
Pringle cans to hold the brushes.
Three-legged easel, gangly as a heron
straddles water and land.
The red-headed woman begins with a grid.
She charts the marsh
like a sailor embarking on a voyage,
finds lavender in a seagull's wing,
saffron in a fallen feather.
A barefoot man leans into the shade
of an acacia. His palette
is a clock of color: cerulean
at eleven, carmine at six. By noon
the marsh will fill again.
The sun casts deeper shades
of blush and brown and in-between,
colors they keep trying to capture.

ALICE KOCIEMBA

Her Bay

I had the landscape in my mind and shoulder and wrist—Helen Frankenthaler

Colors flow from her mind's eye
as precisely as a poet's next line.

Thinned with turpentine, indigo spills
from its can, soaks into the weave like mist.

With a sponge, she spreads the darkest blue
toward the top of the canvas, until it becomes an August sky.

She pours moss-green, squeegees it toward the pulsing blue.
From a punctured coffee can, she drips taupe: fine sand through a sieve.

This bay is inside her, the landscape flowing from her hand.
She drops to one knee, dabs a bit of terracotta—the bay's heart,
                                                    small and fragile.

ADELINE CARRIE KOSCHER

Learning to Live with Water

"Geologically speaking, Cape Cod is little more than a constantly shifting sand bar."
—Brian Morris, WCAI, local NPR station

Spring finds last year's fire road
winter-crumpled into the ocean.
On the radio,
the geology professor says:

We can have buildings or
we can have beaches; we cannot have both.

I walk to the cliff-edge—crane
over the ocean's bitemark,
to see the scar—
I measure, how much, how far,
but cannot fathom what is gone.
A flight of swallows swoops and dances
in the space that was sand.

I want it back:
yesterday, the fire road; I want
sunsets and seals; I want
wild lilies in the woods; I want
to walk along the precipice,
to balance on the edge
of earth and sea, now
and then; I want to hold—
in the cup of my mouth—
the sun and the moon and the summer

132

and my breath forever, but
the ocean has other plans.

Protecting the seashore has left
a dynamic coastline, the professor says.

I bring you to see: the scrub pine torn
from the edge, tossed into the sand
like a bone sucked clean of flesh,
a fishbone or a wishbone—snapped
between two hands—which one is lucky?

In their natural state,
dunes and shorelines come and go.

The professor says, the shoreline
is *supposed* to change, erode, evolve.
That very shoreline—the one that attracted us—
must vanish in order to exist.

We have two choices, he says,
let the water in or try to keep it out.

We are drawn to magenta cloud, jet sea;
moontide and riptide transform us,
reshape us. We cling to a shoreline
crumbling in our hands.

Learning to live with water,
                                        there is a dawning.

Everything, everything is ephemeral—
everything closes, empties, evaporates.
Laughter fades into silence.
Light into darkness.

Even darkness, given time,
disappears.

134

BARRY HELLMAN

Leaving Provincetown

There are no lights on Route 6
so we dream together.

Seaweed and dune
drift over rows
of telephone poles
and Hopper houses,
floors covered
with needles of pine.

A line of cottages
faces the sea,
anchors carved
in their shutters,
curtains blown open
like bathrobes in a wind.

Tea has grown cold
on kitchen tables,
and through each window
the winter beach,
track of a ship
sound of a train.

ALAN FELDMAN

Ashore in Oak Bluffs

The big oaks on the green amid the gingerbread cottages
are shivering and gesturing in the unsettling wind,
    and I'm wondering if the weak link in my anchor chain,

the silvery shackle I used to join it when it snapped
last year in a storm, will hold down there in the harbor
    some miles away. The cottage we're visiting

has a *Wizard of Oz* motif—with tiny Oz figures
half-concealed in the shrubbery. Our friend who owns it
    doesn't care about the story. She's more a conservator

of the previous owner's kitschy taste. And knows
the storm of protest the other cottagers would feel in their hearts
    if she tossed out the figurines, featured

in so many photos. Sometimes she'll find strangers
sitting on the porch, posing. "It's OK," they'll tell her,
    "the owner isn't home." And the wittiest will ask

why the short brick walk leading to the porch isn't yellow.
The Wizard of Oz. The very story that featured in my childhood nightmares
    when I was feverish. With its flying monkeys

and destructive winds. Not like the wind last night,
bathing us in a bugless coolness, as it found its way down the hatch.
    We'd walked from town. And the wind helped us

on the long row from the dock, so the oars dipped gently

into the moonlit current. This must be happiness, I thought,
          when Nan reached over to show me the screen

      of her camera, and I saw my face, lit by the strobe light,
with an extraordinary smile of gleeful surprise. Because everything
          was helping: the wind, the current, Nan pointing the way

      to the anchored boat with its little lantern on its boom.
And then that soothing sleep. Nightmareless. Even the dawn
          fishing boats passing slowly, courteously, making only

      the smallest wake. Such happiness. Like the opening
of a movie, before any violence. Or like the ending of a dream
          when the same breeze hushes the thought

      that the whole island's only temporary. Can you see me,
the tiny figure in the tourists' photos? I'm the one on the porch
          who seems so distracted, listening

      to what the oaks are telling me.

YVONNE

*Charles Speaks of Shearer Cottage**

Back in 1903 in our tight universe
Embroidery was laced with a curse.
Keeping a roof over your head was brave.
Every family middle name was "Slave".

One day I'm chained in a barn and forgotten.
Next day I'm hunting food for the Union.
Day in, day out, calloused hands and sweaty brow.
'Til fist and mind held Hampton know-how.

'Til one day Henrietta and I (both teaching,
Courting, wedding, birthing, always seeking
The Good Lord's narrow path) moved way up North.
Modest, our dreams. Grand, our children's worth.

Modest our means, but I'm a Boston headwaiter,
A man of color—I'm no laughing matter.
We bought a winter home, then a cottage for summer.
Frugal Henrietta. Me? An up-and-comer.

Savvy was Henrietta, not too prissy
For summer laundry duty. Quite necessary
For Boston's nobility. Their extra royal
Treatment, her big business. Not legacy toil.

What legacy deserves summers with a curse?
No embroidered rooms in this wide universe
If your family middle name was "Slave".
So, our gingerbread rooms "To let". Is this brave?

138

Day in, day out, summer bursting with laughter!
Breakfast overflowed like forever after!
Wicker porch lunch and picnics at finger's snap!
Dinners with class! Servitude out! A thunderclap!

Too soon rain fell on our tight paradise.
My Henrietta passed with the mist into sunrise.
Our daughters walked her path without a stumble.
Praise God! May the generations not crumble.

Now I watch the "Daddy boat" glide in all summer.
Let the kids ride the Flying Horses to nowhere!
Round and round, not up and down like the best of us.
Grab the ring. Anybody can. It's only brass.

Round and round, up and down, seems like a curse
Even the best of us must ride in this universe.
What does it matter? Our middle name was slave.
Keeping a happy home is what I call brave.

* The Shearer Cottage, purchased by Charles and Henrietta Shearer from the Baptist
Campground in 1903, is still owned and operated by the family.

SUSAN BERLIN

At the Thrift Shop, Vineyard Haven, Christmas Eve

Nothing else open and an hour to kill
before the ferry delivers my guests, so I go in.

On the radio, Frank and Bing alternately sing.

A woman called Constance greets customers by name as she wrestles
with a stack of puffy winter jackets that keep slipping
from her arms, one by one, asking one customer
how Eli's foot is doing and if, for winter break,
Elizabeth is coming home.

Without enthusiasm, a teenaged girl asks if they have any strollers
for twins. Constance says she's been holding one aside, just in case.

I roam around, the way you do when no one knows you,
looking at this and that as relics of my prior lives rise up to catch
my eye like benign ghosts. An exact replica of my Tiny Tears doll,
the one my cousin Randy made blind, poking out her eyes
with two stiff fingers and a twisted smile.

There's a tortoise shell barrette like the one that held back
my schoolgirl hair. Next to it, an ashtray like the one
my mother bought at Lake Placid, featuring a pelican
with an open beak into which she inserted one burning
cigarette after another, before the disease took hold.

And here's a kid's toy chest like the one I struggled with —
assembly instructions on the floor, screws between my lips —
later to become a coffin for stuffed animals with disabilities

and wooden puzzles, missing pieces.

As they prepare to close, an old woman in a man's
double-breasted coat too broad for her shoulders, snags
her walker on a table leg but rights it, regains control.
She admires a magnifying glass with an ivory handle,
yellowed in the grooves, places it in her basket, reconsiders,
puts it back. It's Christmas Eve. I want to say I'll pay for
whatever she wants but, fearing embarrassment, say nothing.

Constance turns off the radio as the woman makes her way
up front and, from a plastic bag, extracts a scrapbook
padded with quilted fabric—flips it open to reveal
empty slips where photographs are supposed to go.

Hand stitched, she says. *Made it myself, years ago. Now,
give it to someone young enough to fill it.*

JUDITH HERMAN

Your Studio

—for Hela Buchthal, 1922–2013

A gessoed canvas, taut, expectant,
tubes of paint like plump, ripe fruit,
sable brushes lined up, waiting
a Menemsha sunset also ready for you

to make your entrance, set up by the window
and capture the swirling sea, the silver beach
the sky becoming mauve, magenta

as if it were just the other day
and you were at your easel
in your orange painting smock

layering colors across the void
holding the light still.

BROOKS ROBARDS

Anne Vanderhoop

A woman deeply still,
she sits on a stool
at the family business,
perched above the clay cliffs,
active in her silence,
amused by the commerce.

For a minute I see
through her eyes
past an old family
inn, half hidden
in the grasses
under hill's curve
to a shoreline
snaking east
to the horizon,

its dunes not yet
burnished,
the water still
warm but roiled
by a hurricane
passing south.

I look into a universe
tourists come for
but never take home
because it is hers,
and she is part of it,

the beauty without words
of another world
that I want too.

She lives as if
it is contained within
a globe
at the center of
her being

made of sand, of grasses,
cranberry bogs, herring runs,
sky and always
shifting colors
of the sea.

ROBIN SMITH–JOHNSON

Infrequent Flyer

Martha's Vineyard Airport

1.

Here are the long benches
where I rest or try to
what with a nervous stomach
and the gray leaden clouds
stretching outside the window.

The plane looks tiny on the tarmac—
a toy from a Cracker Jack box.
So shiny. It will swallow me.
No child can give it away.
This is the landscape of dreams.

2.

I've heard that planes fall
from the sky, break up
over open water, disappear.
From one moment to the next,
what is becomes only empty space.

In the time it takes to breathe in,
my flight number is called.
Is it necessary to conjure disaster?
I cross to the open door,
feel raindrops on my upturned face.

3.

Seated behind a twenty-something
pilot with a tattoo on his arm,
I grip the leather seat and pray.
Sounding like a tin can in orbit,
the plane roars down the runway

and suddenly lifts clear.
My spirit rises past the Hot Tin Roof,
the gingerbread cottages of Oak Bluffs,
the red cliffs of Aquinnah
and into a long, white funnel of cloud.

DONALD NITCHIE

Beside the Tiasquam

The Tiasquam coils across the flats
like a student's practice handwriting,
curving and back tracking, in no great hurry,
but fast enough to numb your ankles,
mumbling under its leaf mold breath.
Now well stuck in its rut—except
for the dead ends and cut-offs,
wrong turns filling with algae and flies—
it follows the low ground.
Some rivers flow through vast deserts
like long distance runners;
this stream doesn't need to go that far.
It's a self-help tape on infinite loop:
the way it digs itself a bed to ride in;
the way it whistles as it works.

RICHARD FOERSTER

Gay Head

1

Thanks to the Wampanoags' studied indifference,
we've breached the first defense of individuality
and perhaps the last as well—our rainbow
of Izod Lacostes and Calvin Kleins, all the class marks
of the Vineyard's "summer tribe"—and go about bliss-

fully in the buff. For what is flesh between friends
or strangers, if we can doff restraint for an afternoon
with all the flourish of a satin cape?—But not D.,
who's still demure in his boxers, wearing propriety
like a penitential hairshirt. He talks of shame

as something woven on a loom, shuttling across
the generations. It's always seemed a threadbare gift
from a disappointed God—or so the priests
have said in their embroidering. But here
shame flutters on the skin like an airy chiffon,

or at worst like the sudden chill you get
when you think you've locked your keys inside the house,
and there you are, feeling doltish in a business suit,
because you fear the neighbors may be snickering
in the zebra-light of their living rooms.

2

Impermanent as history, this gaudy pentimento

oozes into the Atlantic and the August light
its record of eucalyptus leaves and camel bones.
Abrasive as pumice in the dry sun, it pools
to putty in an afterrain, a rich prismatic
mulch of ferric reds and saffron ocher,
of gray primordial mornings and basalt nights.

The first seamen, with all their mispacked luggage
from home, anemically named this headland
Dover Cliffs. Should we be glad that faith
like theirs erodes, that the monochromatic
certainties refract and are revised,
howsoever diminished and diminishing, like this "gay"
and splendid hemicanyon at the lap of the lapis tide?

3

By easing ourselves into the sun-warm mud
and wallowing like Serengeti beasts, we've become
criminals of leisure, environmental threats.

But this is the sacrament we've come for.
To transubstantiate flesh into stone.
To feel the suck of the earth draw us back.

To hear the quickening sand whisper *Aquinnah*,
the true name. To emerge naked but clothed, knowing
what all those puzzled mud-daubed faces

in the primitive exposures of our dog-eared magazines
were saying to us about crime and shame. And finally
to shiver with this light and dissolve like mist in the waves.

4

The old gent we saw two years ago
shuffled by just now, the same weary packhorse,
burdened—as you said—"with the largest penis
in Christendom." It's still an oddity,
despite his easy pride, outmoded as a pendulum.

For where's his wife? Remember her?—skirted
in a wisp of kelp, an iodine stain that concealed
nothing, least of all the decades
that tugged at her breasts. That summer
at his side, she cradled an armful of shells

as if she were hoarding all the hours of childhood
to be gleaned from this beach. How we chuckled at them
still girdled in the taut confidence of our middle age.
And so here he is now, alone, wearing (can I imagine it?)
neither sorrow nor defiance, but a calm acceptance

of release into a life as malleable as clay.
He's become something runneled with the years that have washed
over him since he first wandered here with her.
And to think we thought them ridiculous, going hand-in-hand
in the soapstone light of these weathered cliffs.

JUDITH HERMAN

Fishmonger

Betsy's in oilcloth apron and high rubber boots
because in a fish market everything is wet
the floor, the dripping baskets, the slithery fish—
and I have been coming here summers for half my life
though she and her family, like the carpenters
masons and farmers, have lived here for generations—
and we are talking about flounder
how it should glisten as it does in her immaculate cases
be firm to the touch, smell like the sea
and I am listening—

                  then I am hauling the fish
from the boats at the dock, myself shucking mussels
I am banding the lobsters to go in the tank
holding up a flounder for a customer to admire
and I've been out with my uncle dragging and longlining
even learned to harpoon

                      and I've gone home at the end of the day
fish scales under my nails and in my hair glittering.

DONALD NITCHIE

02535

In this zip code, trickle-down works
with millionaires for neighbors
up in their waterviews
with their never ending needs—
may their needs never end;

mouse proof the pool house,
leaf-rake the beach,
weed-wack the glacial erratics
and ride-mow the helipad
and golf course—only four holes,
but with a blind at the water hazard.

And the million things that need doing:
money grows on ornamental trees,
on espalier pears and weeping plums,
accrues in wading pools,
in lawns with water systems,
under putting greens, bocce courts,

money wants to run downhill like a water feature,
harness labor like a turbine
and put it on the clock:

woken at 3 a.m. to drive through driving snow
to reset the boiler because the heat went off
then on.

May the heat keep going off then on.
Artwork at a constant 70.

And maybe they'll give you a stock tip,
old car, or big TV—we don't want handouts
but don't mind hand-me-downs.
And may we be grateful for what we receive.

And may the supply-sider dance with the caterer,
and the mow crew admire their work.
And may envy never become your full-time job,
and may external factors never determine
your ultimate worth, even if they do
your rates.

DONALD NITCHIE

Martha's Vineyard vs. Nantucket

Not much between us.
Your two hundred pound linemen,

our tailback like a greased pig.
Your winters even longer than our own,

our superiority of trees.
Same wind-blasted sand dunes and canceled boats,

same tackles and cheerleaders sired by tackles
and cheerleaders. Same empty roads that lead nowhere,

same solitude we thought was all ours.
Some stick around, some go long and don't look back.

Some stumble into trouble and break free, some
don't. Like fraternal twins separated at birth,

we don't recognize each other, rarely speak,
but knock each other down to see who gets up

first. As the winners or losers line up for the shuttle
to the flight or ferry ride home, the home team

waves or turns their backs and everyone
leans on their car horns.

SARAH BROWN WEITZMAN

Off Nantucket Waters

Here the sea storms at the sun, heaving
upward giant black waves that splatter

against the bottom of the sky falling
back into succeeding ridges of rage

that sweep over the shore, over the shore.
The White Elephant Hotel full,

we booked a summer rental cottage
that faced Nantucket Sound

at the gale narrowed point.
On the eighth day you said you'd sail

to town alone, shielding your eyes
against the sun slitting the clouds

to watch a local boy of twelve skim
the foam, round the point and tack

toward the shore. A good wind,
hugging land I'll have an easy trip,

you said, I'll phone you before
I start back. The foolish city dog

our only child ran off down the beach
to gather scents. I went to gather him

but coming back we were waylaid
in the sand flung out momently

from the belly of the sea and sucked
slowly back in again. We might have won

but for a sudden wind. The sky mottled.
We ran before the rain and waited

for your call. Over worsened winds
a neighbor with the simple news instead

that you were dead, lost was what he said.
We've stayed on the dog and I.

The air's October cold, the waves are always
white. I laughed the other day to see a gull

standing on one leg, the other tucked beneath his wing
asleep. Today I found a piece of slate

sea-polished to the color of your eyes.
Each evening the dog and I attend

the sun's descent into the sea, dissolving the difference
between them making them one

red. We watch late until the moon spreads
an arc, tipping each wave dark

silver. But some nights
there is no moon nor stars.

The sky's solid black, the churning
sea concealed.

156

ROBERT FRAZIER

Eclipses of the Heart
(Imaginary Fragments from the Last Diary of Maria Mitchell)

Phebe Mitchell, sister to the noted Nantucket astronomer,
burned several of Maria's journals upon her death in 1889,
because, Phebe claimed, for a Quaker they revealed too much.

1.
Phebe has warned me
about straining my eyes
I can remain only an hour or two at the telescope
and then   nothing

2.
A lucid thought I seemed to hold
tight yesterday has slipped away
like a lover in the morning
and this occultation of yet another faculty
I held so dear
I held like a burning torch before my Vassar girls
saddens me

3.
It seems to have come this far
light years from the stamina I owned
peering into the glass in my youth
my hair is silvered
bones also perhaps
and if I wore the Danish king's medal now
I fear the gold would weigh heavy

4.

I say that for an astronomer to lose her sight
or merely its clarity
is worse than a Friend losing her tongue
for she has other recompenses

5.

Last night I forsook magnification
and accepted the heavens in bold display
standing toward Dionis and the distant shore
to watch the Perseid meteor shower
some distant maiden
combing her hair down
strand by fuzzy strand

MARY FISTER

Nantucket Bluff

Someone must have set it so—
this lone Adirondack chair
on a whiskered bluff
where sea blots sky

beyond the veer.
How many visits to get the angle right?
There had to be a giving over

as sand echoed off
its splintered legs until
the chair sunk no more

and anyone could lean,
then lean back,
watch shells buff to porcelain.

Or was it tossed like so much wrack and spawn,
bladders of kelp,
the sea a rigging
of scallop-shuck and straw?

And what of the lone beachcomber
dallying here
at the bottleneck waist
of the sandbar during low tide?

She walks through
brief tidal pools.

Eddies rush her like run-off,
mollusks scribble beneath sand.

Her tracks fill in
with Arcturus'drift,
risen, glinting.

ALIX ANNE SHAW

Flesh & bone as elements of time

Soil samples taken in Nantucket have revealed a huge pocket of whale oil underlying the island, a legacy of that region's whaling industry. Like petroleum, whale oil does not biodegrade.

The day unfurls itself as we walk by the quarried sea, shoreline where we scan the sky and hunger for constraint. We dream of cord and corset-stay. We dream a prison of bone. Of heart and lungs as a single organ: the life. We dream the body pierced, we dream the flesh peeled back. Of the flesh made liquid, rendered into light.

The pulley heaves its cry as we hoist the sheet of skin, as we watch the flesh in the trypot boil clear. The saturate body spills itself. We sever flesh from flesh. Chrism wells from the head's deep cavity. Oil seeps from the Bible leaf, oil slicks the deck. We move through smoke in a skin of grease and blood. We hang the heavy jawbone, drain its fluid out. Oil runs from the rigging. We turn in our baleen sleep.

Oil covers the shipyard, oil crawls through sand. A lens of oil pools beneath our feet. It spreads through the ground like language—the long, slow, animal pulse that carries across the seafloor, saltdark code. This is the carcass of work we inherit and leave: residue of a creature, flensed in its own viscid light. The oil floats in darkness, drifts through glacial time. The knifeblade rusts, the empty trypot aches. The watchful ocean plies itself. We walk with limbs unbound. As if release were possible. As if the flesh could die. As if the past were tideless, clear, and did not draw us down—to meet its jagged coastline, its blunt and weighty pull.

THOM SLAYTER

The Reluctant Sailor's Lament

"Death to the living, Success to sailors' wives, Long life to the Killers & greasy luck to whales."
Inscription on scrimshaw art of the ship "Susan, off the coast of Japan."
Nantucket Whaling Museum, 1989.

Death to the living
is all I can think of,
lying face down in the gunwales,
cramped up, hating food but hungry.
All is motion, cheerful bustle
of seasoned sailors
in a bracing wind.

Success to sailors' wives.
Maybe the Captain's lady
expects his return
back in Nantucket
and paces the widow's walk.
Or she waits, ready to wail and keen
like a professional mourner.
I have no lady, just visions
of Delilah and Jezebel
to entertain the lust
of my imagination
like Onan in the desert.

Long life to the Killers
for it's sure these voyages devour years.
After all the blood, froth, blubber and oil
there has to be a time

for a quiet space far from the sea
in some wide Western space.
No more can I compass my world
in hammock, hard tack, ditty box,
Bible, candle, and sea chest
or conversations of Sweet Hearth and Home.
I'm tiny in the immensity of ocean
never free to amble anywhere
except this ship's latitude and longitude.

& greasy luck to whales—
Yes, kill them all, soon,
so I can go home.
It's not "Mystical"
as haunted Melville said—
just more work than
I'll ever do again.
Let him have his Moby dreams!
When I get to Cape Cod
I aim to drink my way
to the Berkshires,
plant myself on a mountain.
No **"Susan" on the coast of Japan**
ever again.

JARITA DAVIS

Nantucket Sleigh Ride

The harpoon is thrown and pierces the whale
when someone shouts *Stern all!* They row out
from a tail launching a great wash of water,
thrown like a heavy, wet wall against them, thrown
hard like something they didn't expect to catch and it
throws João back, tumbling him onto his knees.
Their boat is roped to the spear
inside a whale thrashing its escape
and when the vessel lurches forward
João holds on, hears shouts of *Jesus*—his throat
full of salt, then *Good Christ* breathing ocean brine
he holds on, not knowing if the shouts are
curses or prayers or both
and when he chokes on gulps of sea, João knows
he's the one screaming and shuts up now, pressing his mouth
together against the rush, clenching his eyes closed
riding whichever way the boat thrashes and for a moment
no matter how he grips or pushes his feet against what's solid,
he's floating, all of him except his gut
that sinks when the boat lifts the crew in air,
then slams its weight against the surface again
the smack of it through his seat, up the length of his spine
into his shoulders and he holds on, the wet lashing his face
while he tries to hold, still pulling air from water.

It is still and it is dark and João wonders if he is dead.
His wet clothes hang heavy on his limbs. He hears
men talking, then remembers to open his eyes, surprised
he can and surprised he's still alive. The whole crew is alive

and watching the whale at rest. A second harpoon is launched, someone shouts *Stern all!* and João holds his place in the boat.

BARRY HELLMAN

The Last Funeral Home on Nantucket

has closed.

It's not easy to die
on an island
when there's no one
to fold your arms
across your chest,
or put coins
on your eyes.

You'd have to be
shipped by ferry
across the Sound,

cared for by strangers
who can't say
which shirt
or tie to use.

And if it's winter
you could remain
on the mainland
for days,
waiting for the ocean
to calm down:

whoever comes
to the Town Pier
would have time

to think
about your death:
how it happened,
whether it was necessary.

LEAVING THE CAPE & ISLANDS

LORNA KNOWLES BLAKE

Washashores

Saint's Landing, Brewster, Massachusetts

September, and the garden's blown
   and bolted, wren and finch have flown
south, and the sun sets farther down

the bay each passing night. We hate
   the thought of leaving; contemplate
alternatives, as if this bright

and ample season could endure
   beyond the calendar's secure
curfew, but Labor Day is here

and autumn is ready to sue
   for possession. What do we do?
Procrastinate, then pack and go—

my books, your music, linen clothes
   and one more summer is foreclosed
upon by rituals such as these:

stacking canoes and wicker chairs,
   arguing over small repairs
required by weather or the years.

Where is the pulse of a home? What
   is the soul of a house? That
marriage of dwelling and spirit?

Perhaps it's in the flow of tide,
    a herring gull's suspended glide,
the constant birdsong in the shade

reminding us: you are, you are.
    Then, just before we load the car,
the house fills with the airy fire

of sunset and we shroud the place
    in bedding, a green-sprigged embrace
of percale and flannel and fleece.

Is it love, I wonder, when we're done
    or time we're shielding from the sun,
beneath these sheets that we slept on?

LINDA PASTAN

Leaving the Island

We roll up rugs and strip the beds by rote,
summer expires as it has done before.
The ferry is no simple pleasure boat

nor are we simply cargo, though we'll float
alongside heavy trucks—their stick and roar.
We roll up rugs and strip the beds by rote.

This bit of land whose lines the glaciers wrote
becomes the muse of memory once more;
the ferry is no simple pleasure boat.

I'll trade my swimsuit for a woolen coat;
the torch of autumn has but small allure.
We roll up rugs and strips the beds by rote.

The absences these empty shells denote
suggest the losses winter has in store.
The ferry is no simple pleasure boat.

The songs of summer dwindle to one note:
the fog horn's blast (which drowns this closing door).
We rolled up rugs and stripped the beds by rote.
The ferry is no simple pleasure boat.

OFF SEASON: WE LIVE HERE

KATHY BUTTERWORTH

No One Else Is Here

Cisco, Nantucket

The sea pulls
my watery body so close
each step
leaves a mark in wet sand.

A young man prepares
with careful execution
his wet suit and kite
taking time to smooth them.

You have to understand it's winter.
The beach is steep and shortened.
No one else is here.

He wades in knee deep
lets his kite shoot up
flies in the frenzy
straight out

as if he will leave here
and in a moment arrive
on a distant shore.

A ripple of water
washes against my boot,
dampens the hem of my jeans.
I weigh my chances for escape.

DONALD NITCHIE

Happy Hour at the Ritz Cafe

The Season, which is over, burrows
into itself like a mole in the lawn.
The rich have departed.
Defeat permeates the room.

The week's Cases in District Court
huddle along the bar, plotting their next
marked lane violations, Class D possessions,
(Insert Your Crime Here).

Our resident smuggler
and unemployed hustler
orbits three housecleaners
in tightening circles.

Trophy homes rule the horizon—
flotsam left high by departing tides—
as we second- and third-home-
less crouch in their shadows

and cry in our beers. Contractor husbands
("just on my way home"), Circuit Ave. regulars,
charmers, pub-crawlers—all are drawn in
to the stifling warmth

of their own kind: the flushed cheeks
and vacant stares of the marathon
spongers, propped up on bar stools
like Exhibit A also-rans.

Don't forget the barmaid—she calls this ship-
wreck home. And Banned-For-Life, our favorite
reprobate and local hero who swears
he stormed the sands

at Normandy, hot-foots it out on the sidewalk
like the class clown, making faces at us all.
He's the joke we get too well,
calling us to scale

the castle walls, send the nobles packing.
The Class War begins tonight! But first there's this
scalloper on my right, egging for a fight, he
doesn't care with whom.

MEAGHAN QUINN

In the Back Booth at Bobby Byrne's Pub

it's March which means everyone's getting clean & sober on the Cape
carpenters unveil their splintered hands   sober house girls hide their second day hair
under Sox caps   bounce their little ones in the back of St. Anthony's Church

     Strange shit happens here my buddy says   no one talks about it   maybe he's right
once the boats winterize & the Oysters Rockefeller grow rubbery hoards of us are still here

mopping the movie theaters

naming constellations   carpooling to the clinic   minding the Main Street shops
gossiping about the dude who got his leg chopped off in a wood chipper   later we'll log on
to Facebook to see which 24 year old died of an overdose   without fail   every week   without
fail

my buddy etches his ambitions into scratch tickets as we snag a booth   while beside us old
timers eat supper in the snuggery   where God lurks somewhere between a waitress and a
bowl of chowder

ROBIN SMITH–JOHNSON

Loaves and Fishes

I'd seen the ad for weeks:
Food Pantry, Mashpee Baptist Church.
It was not what I wanted, but one morning
there was no food in the cupboards.
I set out in my old clunker through the snow,
cold air coming in where the window wouldn't shut.
I had promised my children something for their lunch.
Now I could only hold my breath.
After parking in the back, I tripped on ice.
Inside, I was given a paper bag and a request.
Only one of every item, so I loaded up:
a loaf of bread, a box of mac & cheese, some milk.
The food and staples were lined up on long tables.
It was bounty but controlled in size.
As I filled my sack, the heavens opened up.
The most powerful, glorious voice I ever heard
came from the floor above, a choir perhaps.
There was more here to fill my needs.
Forgetting my cares,
I returned home. For this day,
it was enough.

JUDITH PARTELOW

Cape Cod Life

Cape Codders
who live by the sea
and look at stars

breathing salt air—
painting pretty scenes
of wind-blown hair

aren't the Cape Codders
who sleep in cars
and never see the sea

for necessity
of keeping themselves fed
or finding their child a bed

and not enough time in the day
to while away
and sing of its charms

as they seek any jobs
to buy clothes and fuel;
to keep warm.

DIANE HANNA

For Those Who Stay

It is winter in Cotuit, my village cradled by the sea.
North wind scours gray shingles, scrubs away all
traces of summer ease, bleaches the air white
as frozen sheets.

In humble cottages, sand shirrs across bare floors.
Ghosts hungry for jelly sandwiches, settle into wing chairs
by the cold fireplace, listen for laughter caught in wall
cracks, bureau drawers, linen closets stuffed with towels.

Summer houses shiver and sigh, faceless windows stormed
with snow. We walk by, whisper condolences to plates in musty
cupboards, dried-up spigots, a timed lamp in a corner, unslept-in
beds, yellowed fliers stuck in doors.

We pass a single crow on the beach, walk up Main Street, past
library, post office, busy tavern to home, its furnace breathing,
its leftovers in the fridge, frying pan in the sink, thirsty geraniums,
vacuum cleaner left in the hall.

After a storm, when there is no light, no heat, when doors
seal with drifts, silence works its way into the heart, speaks
of an exquisite loneliness human as blood and bone, winter's
poem for those who stay.

RICK SMITH

Hyannis, 1982

We're in Hyannis.
It's cold.
My '65 VW
with California plates
gets me to the lot
behind the Trailways depot.
It's 11 p.m.
And January.
I got a $100 bill
from some doctor up on Liam Lane
who wants to get high.
I leave the engine running.
The lot is empty.
The 10:42 to Fall River, Pawtucket
and Providence is running late, but it's running:
tail lights fading out on Rt. 6.
A guy with a Red Sox cap
under his hoodie,
slips out
from the back of a building.
That's who I'm looking for.
I give him the hundred.
He hands me the coke
in a paper bindle.
I take a little taste
and pull away.
The heater hasn't worked for months
but now, I won't need it.
"One Thing Leads to Another"

184

comes on the radio.
I love that song.
I love this night.

You know,
Hyannis wasn't such a bad place
till the wrong kind of people
started moving in.

MICHAEL SHAPIRO

Winter Roads

I.
I drive down Route 28 in Yarmouth on this
last Sunday of the year:
past empty motel parking lots,
bereft miniature golf courses,
the shuttered salt-water taffy stand,
hibernating restaurants that await
the tourist families of May.

The merest of overcasts turns the already pale
year-end sun into a thin gruel of little comfort

II.
New Year's Eve morning—Bridge Road, Eastham
past the derelict water tower and the old cemetery
with its fence of rough-hewn granite and galvanized pipe
slate grave markers sinking ever deeper into
still soft earth—a reminder of our entropic destiny

Off to the west scudding clouds dim the sun
Cape Cod Bay turns the slate of the gravestones

III.
Driving south on Bridge Road,
on the first Saturday of the new year
bay to the west, salt marsh off eastward
mist and low cloud on a mild day blur boundaries:
sea from cloud, horizon from sky.

186

What happened from what might have been,
what is desired from what will come to be

VALERIE LAWSON

Winter Rental

The last surge carried the cottage across the street.
It lay canted, a fifty-foot sloop leaning on it
like a drunken sailor, rigging caught in the weathervane.
Cleared of wreckage and reset on FEMA rated pilings,
its defiant windows still face the sea. Perched
on jacks, a half-scraped boat waits for spring.

When the bad storms come watchers often find one
passed out cold at the high-water mark.
Winter rental folk, drawn to the hearth
in the off season stay until rugosa roses peel off
scratchy winter hips and send out pale green shoots.

Offshore the seals sing their far-away songs
their bobbing heads shining like stars in the belly of a wave.
There is a season before storm, when screen door stiles
gently kiss the casing, the hinges quiet, the spring untested.
Come foul weather, the unlatched door is the first to go,
catching relentless winds, flying like a kite without a tail.

MARY BERGMAN

Provincetown, Late October, 6 am

Venus is rising and
I have been sweeping
sand for hours.
Underfoot, each tiny grain like a glass sliver.
We used to get lost out here,
imagine we were astronauts exploring the pockmarked surface of the moon.
Searching for seconds of weightlessness, tumbling end over end in the surf.
Do you still wake from those dreams with sand in your hair?
He said, there's nothing here to steal but solitude
but if the mosquito bites on my ankles are any indication
then I am not really alone in the dunes.
You think they would all be gone by now, overwintering somewhere warmer.
But they are proving as hearty as the pitch pine.
Still, I'm certain there are more dead than living in the dunes.
Ashes scattered along the shore,
or buried down in No-Hands-Valley,
and a century of countless sailors, wrecked on the bar.
Surfmen patrolled this backshore,
their lanterns throwing long shadows on compass grass.
And me?
I am listening to the wind and the coyotes howl,
each trying to outdo the other.

MARTIN I. LEVINE

November

Down at the Captain's Table
the old Portuguese fisherman is drinking
to the coming of the dead-eyed

winter. A coyote and a cold wind,
hard with hunger, move through
the lean pickings of the feeding

tide, abandoned rose hips, pale
dune grasses, rows of empty summer
cottages, and the edge of the brittle

salt marsh, as the winter buttons up
the frost-whipped beach
like a man closed shut.

I stop at the red cottage
where the coldness echoes through the eaves
where a broken mantis lies

where no one is sitting down to breakfast
where your naked feet do not run wet
through the rooms

where unsoiled sheets do not rise bittersweet
on your chocolate brown nipples
where your fragrance does not fill the room

where there are no little ceremonies
where the stars mirror the dark sea

190

JENNIFER ROSE

East End Postcard

Provincetown, December

I love the mosaic these shacks make
as they gerrymander the air for their views
of the harbor. Some tiptoe on stilts
right down to the water, precarious
as drag queens in Fifties stilettos.
An unleashed Labrador studies the jetties.
Laundry lines shiver with year-rounders' skivvies.
At night Route 6 wears a fabulous topaz
necklace on the décolleté bay, the marina,
a tiara of lights near where I stay.
What life might I live were I brave enough
to love the right woman? Hourly all of us fall
in the circle of P-town's sole church bell—
the gulls, quaint cottages of lovers, and me.
Time has no tourists, unlike the sea,
or love, although unwillingly.

MARY OLIVER

Coming Home

When we're driving, in the dark,
on the long road
to Provincetown, which lies empty
for miles, when we're weary,
when the buildings
and the scrub pines lose
their familiar look,
I imagine us rising
from the speeding car,
I imagine us seeing
everything from another place—the top
of one of the pale dunes
or the deep and nameless
fields of the sea—
and what we see is the world
that cannot cherish us
but which we cherish,
and what we see is our life
moving like that,
along the dark edges
of everything—the headlights
like lanterns
sweeping the blackness—
believing in a thousand
fragile and unprovable things,
looking out for sorrow,
slowing down for happiness,
making all the right turns
right down to the thumping

barriers to the sea,
the swirling waves,
the narrow streets, the houses,
the past, the future,
the doorway that belongs
to you and me.

NOTES TO THE POEMS

To the Cape

"Route 6," Stanley Kunitz: Route 6 is the main highway on Cape Cod, also called the Mid-Cape highway. Parallel routes include Route 28 and Route 6A.

"Bourne Bridge," Alice Kociemba: The Cape Cod Canal is a man-made waterway that connects Cape Cod to the mainland. The canal opened on a limited basis in 1914 and was completed in 1916. It was later widened and deepened, and by 1940 it had become the widest sea-level canal in the world. The first Bourne Bridge was built between 1910-1913 and later replaced with the present bridge in 1935. It is one of two bridges that span the canal; the Sagamore Bridge to its north also opened in 1935. For Cape Codders and visitors alike, the canal has become the unofficial demarcation between the mainland and the Cape. The experience of seeing the glimmering waters of the canal serves as the symbolic entrance to Cape Cod.

Origin Stories

"Doane Rock," Rich Youmans: Doane Rock is a huge boulder that can be found on the grounds of the Cape Cod National Seashore in Eastham (one mile past the Salt Pond Visitor Center and Coast Guard Beach). The Laurentide Ice Sheet was one of the largest glacial sheets that covered the Earth 20,000 years ago, before it began retreating as temperatures rose. As it retreated over millennia, it shaped the Cape's terrain and left behind huge boulders. Deposited 18,000 to 12,000 years ago, Doane Rock stands 18 feet high—it is the largest exposed boulder on Cape Cod—and extends below the ground another 12 feet. It was named after Deacon John Doane, an original Eastham settler. Like many early settlers, he came to the Cape from Plymouth Colony around 1644. The former Doane homestead is located nearby, although only its foundation remains.

"Fireball at the Powwow," Mary Clare Casey: Since 1922, the annual Wampanoag Powwow has traditionally been held on the Fourth of July weekend. It is a homecoming celebration for tribal members and includes much drumming and dancing. One of the main attractions of the three-day event is Fireball—a medicine game played by Native men and boys. The ritual resembles a soccer game, with a ball made of old sheets and rags that is stuffed into a sphere of chicken wire and soaked in kerosene. It is also part of a healing ceremony where players offer their courage for people who are seriously ill.

"This Language, This Blood, This Land," Rich Youmans: The Wôpanâak Language Reclamation Project began in 1993 under the direction of Jessie Little Doe Baird of Mashpee, who was inspired after she had several dreams of native ancestors speaking an unknown language. There had been no fluent speakers of Wampanoag for over 150 years, and it is the first American Indian language to be reclaimed with no living speakers. In her testimony to the U.S. Senate Committee on Indian Affairs, Ms. Baird noted that one of the Wôpanâak words, "nupunuhshâm," means "both 'I have fallen down' and 'I have lost my land rights,' that my feet ... have been removed from me." Just as the land was not separate from the body, so too were the land and the language inextricably linked. The reclamation was based in part on a 1663 Bible translated into Wôpanâak, as well as other legal documents written in the language.

"On the Magnetism of Certain Spots on Earth, like Provincetown," Elizabeth Bradfield: Governor William Bradford (1590-1657) was the governor of Plymouth Colony for thirty years. A passenger on the Mayflower, he was one of the signers of the Mayflower Compact and is best known for leading the Pilgrims and founding Plymouth Colony. His first wife Dorothy fell overboard from the dock of the Mayflower during one of the early expeditions to select a settlement.

"Thoreau's *Cape Cod*," Susan Donnelly: Henry David Thoreau (1817-1862) was a naturalist, poet, and philosopher. He decided to trek across Cape Cod in 1849 (two years after his famous stint at Walden Pond) and made several more trips between 1849 and 1855—having fallen in love with what he saw, he planned to study the Cape's people, flora, and fauna. During his trip in 1849, Thoreau walked the outer beach from Eastham to Provincetown in four days. His book, *Cape Cod*, was published in 1865 and chronicled his stay. The book began as a series of essays later compiled into book form. The famous quote from his book reads, "A man may stand there and put all America behind him."

Scenes from the Cape & Islands

"At the Sandwich Glass Museum," Sara Letourneau: In 1825, a Boston businessman, Deming Jarves, started the Sandwich Glass Company. At its height, the company employed 600 people. In 1858, the company began showing less profit, so Jarves took his son, John W. Jarves, and started a new company down the road: The Cape Cod Glass Works. The Glass Works' furnaces were stopped on the same day that Deming Jarves died in 1869. The Sandwich Glass Company, however, continued making glass until it was shut down in 1888. The Cape Cod Glass Works was taken over by John Charles DeVoy, who had an interest in making variegated colored glass. During the early part of the 20th century, the glass-making industry died out. In 1907, the Sandwich Historical Society was founded, and it held its first glass exhibit in 1925. Today, the Sandwich Glass Museum collection holds more than 5,000 pieces produced between 1825 and 1888.

"Abandoned Bog, West Falmouth," Laurel Kornhiser: Cape Cod has been home to many industrial endeavors. In the eighteenth and nineteenth centuries, industries sprang up that included tanning, salt works, glass works, and cranberry growing. This area was well suited to the growing of cranberries due to its long frost-free growing season, acidic peat soils, and good water supply. The first cranberries were harvested in 1816 by Captain Henry Hall in Dennis. By 1854, there were cranberry bogs in most Cape Cod towns. Many early Cape immigrants worked in the bogs and became part of the local population. In addition, the Wampanoag Indians used the wild cranberries for healing rituals. Cranberries are still harvested locally to this day. Two poems in this collection reference cranberry harvest: "Harvesting a Return" by Jarita Davis and "Union Street Bog, Yarmouth" by Paula Trespass.

"At the Edge of the Sea with Rachel Carson," Frank Finale: Rachel Carson (1907-1964) was an author and conservationist best known for her groundbreaking book *Silent Spring*, about the dangers of chemical pesticides (like DDT) on the natural world. After graduating from the Pennsylvania College for Women (now Chatham University) in 1929, she went on to receive her MA in zoology at Johns Hopkins University in 1932. She studied at the Woods Hole Marine Biological Laboratory, first in 1929 and later in the summer of 1932 as a beginning investigator in zoology. At the prime of her career, she worked as a writer and biologist with the U.S. Bureau of Fisheries (now the Fish and Wildlife Service) in Washington, D.C. At the time her book *The Sea Around Us* came out in 1951, she spent July

196

and August in Woods Hole. She died of cancer in 1964 and was posthumously awarded the Presidential Medal of Freedom in 1980.

"Penikese Island Triptych," Cliff Saunders, and "A Further Explication of Irony,"
Elizabeth Bradfield: Penikese Island is located in the Elizabeth Islands, a chain of small islands extending southwest from the southern coast of Cape Cod, about fifteen miles from Woods Hole. During the early 1900s, Penikese was home to a leper colony. Those stricken with the disease were shunted to this wind-swept, seventy-four-acre island and held there for the rest of their lives. Opened in 1905, the colony was one of only three in the United States (the other two were in Louisiana and California). Those sick from the disease were brought from other places and were often exiles from countries such as Japan, Greece, Portugal, and Russia. When the colony shut down in 1921, it had fifty patients, most of them immigrants. Penikese Island later became home to an alternative school for troubled boys, which ran through 2011. Today it is a haven for naturalists.

"Harvesting a Return," Jarita Davis: Among the first immigrants to arrive on Cape Cod were those from Portugal and the Azores. Many moved to Provincetown, where they became a major part of the fishing industry. A large number of Portuguese also moved to New Bedford to work in the whaling industry. Many immigrated from the Cape Verde Islands seeking greater job opportunities; they became fishermen, farmers, whalers, and workers in the cranberry bogs. The Portuguese families who came in the mid-1800s were important to the social, economic, and cultural life of these shores.

"Kennedy Compound, Hyannis Port," David R. Surette: On Jan. 8, 1929, millionaire Joseph Kennedy purchased a cottage at 28 Marchant Ave. in Hyannis Port to support his expanding family. Intended as a summer residence for his wife and their nine children, it became a special place for the Kennedy family, growing into a compound with three clapboard houses, sprawling lawns, and the nearby waters of Nantucket Sound. It was the site where John F. Kennedy set up his presidential campaign in 1960. Later, the president liked to slip away to the compound for rest and recreation. John F. Kennedy often referred to the compound as his true home. It was here, he said, he felt most in touch with nature, his friends and family, and his heritage.

"The Law Ghosts," Susan Donnelly: The Barnstable Inn on Route 6A has a reputation for being a home to ghosts. Built in 1716, the place has seen several owners and has allegedly been the site of many hauntings. The most famous is the "waiter ghost," who is dressed in old colonial clothes and moves about with a towel over his arm. The ghost of Captain John Gray, a former owner, is said to slam doors. The house is also known for the "phantom fires" that suddenly appear in the fireplace. Another story about the house is that after responding to a fire there in the 1970s, several firemen reported seeing a woman, dressed in an old-fashioned gown, staring down at them from a third-floor window. The inn is sometimes called the House of 11 Ghosts and is thought to be one of the most haunted places on Cape Cod.

"E Is for Edward," Deirdre Callanan: One of Cape Cod's most beloved and eccentric residents was artist and writer Edward Gorey. He was born in 1925 in Chicago and, after graduating from Harvard in 1950, began illustrating book covers for Doubleday. Although he tried to jumpstart a writing career, he couldn't finish the novels he began, so he worked on small books. After living in New York City, Gorey eventually found his place on the Cape—the Elephant House, now the Edward Gorey House, on Strawberry Lane in Yarmouth Port. He lived there until his death in 2000. While he lived on the Cape, Gorey was instrumental in staging many of his stories in local theaters. He was a master of the art of the macabre. "E is for "Edward" contains multiple references to the places and people Gorey knew on the Cape.

Line 1: Cape Cinema in Dennis, Massachusetts.
Line 2: Rockwell Kent's mural on the auditorium ceiling of the Cape Cinema; it represents heavens and constellations.
Line 6: Helen Pond and Herbert Senn, set designers for many plays at the Cape Playhouse in Dennis.
Line 7: George Balanchine was artistic director of the New York City Ballet from 1948 until his death in 1983.
Line 8: Gorey's house, situated at 8 Strawberry Lane, Yarmouth Port.
Line 11: Jack's Outback Restaurant in Yarmouth Port. Gorey was a regular patron who, with Pond, Senn, and a few others, formed what his friend and protégé Brian Rice called a "nerdy, intellectual, artsy Rat Pack."
Line 12: John and Eve Carey, owners of Eden Hand Arts in the late '60s, invented the "Cape Cod Bracelet." They were part of the group at Jack's Outback.
Line 16: An invitation for a friend's wedding.
Line 22: Gorey designed the set for *Dracula*, which was performed by the Nantucket Stage Company in 1973 and, after limited engagements in Boston, premiered on

Broadway in October 1977, just before Halloween. Gorey won a Tony Award for costume design.

Lines 26-28: Refers to characters and episodes in Gorey's *The Gashleycrumb Tinies* (1963), an alphabetical catalog of 26 children's deaths.

Lines 29-31: Refers to characters and episodes in Gorey's *The Willowdale Handcar* (1962).

Lines 32-33: Figbash, a "disturbing, eyeless being," debuted in Gorey's book *The Raging Tide* (1987) and became one of his most renowned characters. It echoes Max Ernst's creation Loplop.

"Over the Shoal, Bass River," Phyllis Henry-Jordan: The Beetle Cat is a one-design sailing dinghy. Built predominantly with oak and cedar, it was adapted from the traditional Cape Cod catboats designed for fishing in shallow waters.

"Roaming the Aisles at the Brewster General Store," Diane Hanna: The Brewster General Store is a familiar landmark for Cape Codders. Originally built as a church in 1852, it was converted to a general store in 1866. The new owner, William K. Knowles, removed the church steeple and added storefront windows. Over the years, the store has had a series of owners. It is a place where locals meet for their morning coffee on the bench outside or, during winter months, around the coal-burning stove inside. The store is a reminder of bygone times, where visitors come for the penny candy, souvenirs, and knick-knacks. There is even a Nickelodeon player piano.

"Eating Meltaways in Harwich Port," Barbara Crooker: Bonatt's Bakery was a long-time institution in Harwich Port and the home of the "meltaway," a sweet pastry shaped like a horseshoe. The business was started by AJ and Rose Bonatt in 1941. Later, Jim Bonatt took over from his parents and ran it with his wife, Alice, whom he married in 1977. They each had six children from previous marriages, so they blended their large families. When Jim died in 1978, Alice decided to keep the business going. Four years later, she sold the business and spent thirty years working for the town of Harwich as an emergency dispatcher. After she retired in 2010, she bought the bakery in 2012 and ran it until 2017, when the work became too much.

"Bird Carver," Robin Smith-Johnson: Bird carver A. (Anthony) Elmer Crowell (1862-1952) was one of Cape Cod's most notable figures. From an early age he was interested in nature and wildlife, and at age 12 his father gave him his first 12-gauge shotgun. His love of hunting eventually led to his affinity for bird carving. In 1912, he started carving full time, working out of a small shop in his home in East Harwich. Unlike other decoy carvers of that time, Crowell signed his pieces. This practice helped to carry his name beyond Cape Cod and build his fame as an outstanding craftsman. He paid meticulous attention to detail, both in the carving of bills and feathers and in the painting of feathers onto his decoys. In September 2007, two of Crowell's birds, a pin-tail drake and a Canada goose, sold for a record $1.13 million.

"Chatham's Seals at South Beach," Linda Haviland Conte: Cape Cod is home to thousands of seals mostly located on Monomoy Island off South Chatham. According to recent studies, Cape Cod now has the largest number of gray seals on the East Coast, as many as ten to twelve thousand. Some experts speculate that the ever-growing seal population has attracted white sharks, which have been spotted in waters all along the Outer Cape, including Wellfleet and Chatham. The sharks go where there is abundant food for them to eat. It is also possible that climate change has played a part in this migration. It appears sharks and seals are here to stay.

"Henry Beston's Outermost House," Maxine Susman, and "The Outermost House," Sharon Tracey: Henry Beston (1888-1968) grew up in Quincy, Massachusetts, and was educated at Harvard. After college, he served with the ambulance corps during World War I. Later, he became a writer and editor. In September 1926, he went for what he thought would be a two-week vacation to a small cabin he had built a year earlier, in the dunes two miles south of the Coast Guard Station at Nauset. He fell in love with the place and stayed for a year to chronicle his experiences living by the sea. The resulting book, *The Outermost House,* was published in the fall of 1928 and became a classic of literary nature writing. The Outermost House was designated a national literary landmark shortly before Henry's death, but ultimately it was swept away in raging seas during the Blizzard of '78.

"Edward Hopper's Color Notes for Route 6, Eastham," Joseph Stanton: Edward Hopper (1882-1967) was an American realist artist and printmaker. He grew up in Nyack, New York, showing artistic talent at a young age, and studied at the New York School of Art and Design. When he worked at an advertising agency in 1905, he realized he didn't like illustration. He traveled and worked in Europe several times and was drawn to urban and architectural scenes. On a summer painting trip to Gloucester, Massachusetts, he met and married fellow artist Josephine Nivison. In 1930, the couple rented a house in South Truro.

They subsequently spent every summer there, eventually building a summer home in 1934. Many of his paintings feature Cape settings including "House on Dune Edge" (1931) and "Cold Storage Plant" (1934). He died in his studio in New York City on May 15, 1967.

"Eastham Turnips, November" Gail Mazur: Common in Eastern Europe, turnips were grown in Colonial America and became a dietary staple in the 1800s. Conditions in Eastham were ideal for growing the finicky vegetable – not too hot nor too cold. The tradition of holding the Eastham Turnip Festival each November began in 2003. Sponsored by the Eastham Public Library, it's held each year at Nauset Regional High School and features a turnip-shucking contest, children's activities, music, and a host of vendors. (Note: The festival was held virtually in 2020.)

"Booth #51 at the Wellfleet Flea Market," Alexis Ivy: The Wellfleet Flea Market is located at the Wellfleet Drive-in, Route 6; it's open on weekends from mid-April through early fall, with additional days during July and August. Since it debuted in 1974 (17 years after the drive-in opened), the flea market has been a destination for treasure hunters and day trippers. Vendors come from all over New England and rent tables where they ply their wares. It's a place to look for antique post cards or baseball cards, old books, furniture, as well as jewelry, records, handmade crafts, and much more.

"Marconi Station: South Wellfleet," Steven Bauer: Born in Bologna, Italy, in 1874, the famed inventor and engineer Guglielmo Marconi began conducting experiments with wireless radio signaling in 1895. In 1896, he was granted a patent for a system of wireless telegraphy and was able to demonstrate the system's ability to transmit radio signals. His first successful transatlantic transmission, in 1901, was sent from Poldhu in Southern England to St. John's, Newfoundland, 1,700 miles away. He moved to Cape Cod in 1912 and built four 210-foot towers in the Wellfleet bluffs. On January 18, 1903, the first transmission between the United States and Europe took place there. The transmission took just four minutes and contained greetings from President Theodore Roosevelt to King Edward of Great Britain, who responded in kind.

"Hamblen Farm Morning, Wellfleet," Paula Erickson: In Daniel Lombardo's book *Wellfleet, A Cape Cod Village*, the author notes that Benjamin Hamblen (1692-1737) built the first house where Hamblen Farm would later stand. Hamblen, who made his living on whaling voyages, suffered a terrible fate while at sea, as Lombardo recounts: "A large whale

201

had been killed and brought to the side of the ship. 'As the hands were hoisting the blubber into the hold, the runner of the block gave way, and fell with great force, on the head of a man, who stood underneath—Benjamin Hamblen—and instantly killed him.'" Hamblen's descendants carried on the name and **Hamblen Farm** has been an important part of Wellfleet's history. It is no longer a working farm, but the buildings are still there.

"An Intermission," Brendan Galvin: The Atlantic Flyway is a major north-south flyway for migratory birds in North America. The route generally starts in Greenland, then follows the Atlantic Coast south to the tropical areas of South America and the Caribbean. It spans more than 3,000 miles.

"Late Bus," Keith Althaus: This poem references the panels depicting old Portuguese women (all fishermen's wives) that line the side of a building on the town wharf in Provincetown. The five photographs were taken by Norma Holt in the 1970s and honored those women who stayed home and raised families while their men went out to sea. The black and white photos depict Almeda Segura, Eva Silva, Mary Jason, Bea Cabral, and Frances Raymond. The installation, titled "They Also Faced the Sea," wasn't expected to last long but survived for twelve years albeit very faded. The photographs were then reprinted and reinstalled in 2015.

"From the Pilgrim Monument," Keith Althaus: The Pilgrim Monument in Provincetown commemorates the first landfall of the Pilgrims in 1620 and the signing of the Mayflower Compact in Provincetown Harbor. Construction took place between 1907 and 1910: President Theodore Roosevelt laid the cornerstone on August 20, 1907, while President William H. Taft led the dedication ceremony after the monument's completion on August 5, 1910. Designed by architect Willard Thomas Sears, it is patterned after the Torre Del Mangia in Siena, Italy, and is the tallest all-granite structure in the United States, rising 252 feet, 7.5 inches (77 meters), 350 feet above sea level. The walk to the top takes 116 steps or about 10 minutes to climb. The Pilgrim Monument and Provincetown Museum is Cape Cod's oldest non-profit and cultural institution. (pilgrim-monument.org).

"Pilgrim Spring," Fred Marchant: The Pilgrim Spring Trail is one of two trails at Pilgrim Heights near Truro (the other is Small's Swamp Trail), at the northern end of the Cape Cod National Seashore. This trail leads to the freshwater spring the Pilgrims discovered when they landed at Provincetown before sailing to Plymouth. The trail is popular for its beautiful views and easily walkable distance.

"Province Lands Dunes," Rosalind Pace: In the early 1900s, artists flocked to Provincetown for its thriving artists' colony and unique ambiance. Many of these early residents spent time in rustic shacks on the dunes, some of which were originally life-saving huts from the 1890s. Today, nineteen dune shacks remain intact, with eighteen belonging to the National Park Service. The shacks are situated along the back shore of Provincetown and Truro and are part of the Peaked Hill Bars Historic District. Former residents include Harry Kemp, well-known in Provincetown as the "poet of the dunes," and playwright Eugene O'Neill, who came to stay in a dune shack every summer until 1924. Other famous artists and writers who used the shacks included playwright Susan Glaspell, journalist John Reed, arts patron Mabel Dodge, and journalist/novelist Mary Heaton Vorse. With sweeping views of the ocean, the artists spent their time in creative work or relaxation. The shacks are now registered as historic landmarks.

"Promised Land," Egan Millard: Incorporated as a town in 1727, Provincetown initially grew as a fishing and whaling center, until the 1898 Portland Gale storm sunk dozens of vessels and left the local industry in tatters. Consequently, many artists took over abandoned buildings and a thriving arts colony began. In the mid-1960s, counter-culture groups thrived because of the low rents and agreeable milieu. In the 1970s the town's gay population exploded during the summer months, and Provincetown has since become known as an LGBTQ mecca, with businesses catering to same-sex clientele and the Carnival Parade—a week-long celebration of LGBTQ life—a highlight of the summer season.

"Homage to the *Patricia Marie,*" Alice Kociemba: The scallop-laden *Patricia Marie* sank with all hands aboard Oct. 24, 1976, the worst night for the Provincetown fishing fleet in over 60 years. The boat went down about three miles off Nauset Light in heavy seas and rain. Only the body of vessel captain William King was immediately recovered — the next day, on a buoy. Immediately after the sinking, the crew remained missing and presumed dead. They were Morris Joseph; his son, Alton; Walter Marshall; Richard Oldenquist; Robert Zawalick; and Ernest Cordeiro.

"Blue Skies," M. Brockett-Devine: Sitting at the tip of Cape Cod, Provincetown has always been an important fishing port. Although the local fleet has declined in recent years, commercial fishing still plays an important role in the town's life and culture. The Provincetown Portuguese Festival and the Blessing of the Fleet are seventy-year traditions held on the last Sunday of June. The festival celebrates Portuguese culture and concludes with boats decked out in their finest at MacMillan Pier receiving the annual blessing from a Catholic bishop.

"Atlantis: Michael's Dream," Mark Doty: During the early 1980s, young gay men began dying of a terrible illness: AIDS (Acquired immunodeficiency syndrome), the most advanced stage of HIV (human immunodeficiency virus). The virus attacks cells that help the body fight infection, making a person more vulnerable to other infections and diseases. The first cases were diagnosed in Provincetown in 1982. All told, by 1996, AIDS had claimed 385 Provincetown citizens (10 percent of the town's population). The town came together in support of the AIDS victims and their families, and many out-of-state gay men moved to Provincetown to spend their last days in a caring, compassionate environment. In June 2018, the Provincetown AIDS Memorial was unveiled and dedicated to honor those who died.

"Mary Oliver, Reading," Catherine R. Cryan: Mary Oliver (1935-2019) was one of the most popular and influential American poets in recent memory. Her poems are based on a quiet study of nature. As a young woman, she was drawn to the poetry of Edna St. Vincent Millay and lived briefly at Millay's homestead (Steepletop in Austerlitz, New York), helping Millay's sister to organize the poet's papers. It was here Oliver met her lifelong partner, Molly Malone Cook. After moving to Provincetown with Cook, Oliver wrote many of the poems that made her famous. She lived in Provincetown for over fifty years and became a vital member of the community; in fact, she was sometimes called "The Bard of Provincetown." Although she moved to Florida near the end of her life, people still remember her walking the streets of Provincetown with her dogs.

"Stanley's Garden," Cathie Desjardins: Stanley Kunitz (1905-2006) became the tenth U.S. Poet Laureate in 2000 at ninety-five years old. With his third wife, Elise Asher, he divided his time between Manhattan and Provincetown. A tireless promoter of poetry, he founded the Poets House in Manhattan and the Fine Arts Work Center in Provincetown. His last book *The Wild Braid, A Poet Reflects on a Century in the Garden*, pays tribute to another of his passions. He was a beloved part of the Provincetown community and is buried in the Provincetown Cemetery.

"Her Bay," Alice Kociemba: At the beginning of the twentieth century, artists began to flock to the Outer Cape and soon transformed the landscape. Among them were Hans Hofmann (1880-1966), a German-born American painter who was well known as both an artist and a teacher (his work was considered a breakthrough in abstract expressionism for its bold use of color), and Jackson Pollock (1912-1956), a major figure in the abstract expressionist movement who became known for his technique of pouring or splashing liquid household paint onto a horizontal surface. Both taught in Provincetown, and their students included many notable artists, including Helen Frankenthaler (1928-2011). Long recognized as one of the great American artists of the twentieth century, Frankenthaler was eminent among the second generation of postwar American abstract painters, and she is widely credited for playing a pivotal role in the transition from Abstract Expressionism to Color Field painting. Through her invention of the soak-stain technique, she expanded the possibilities of abstract painting, enabling her to better express spontaneity (she said that "a really good picture looks as if it's happened all at once"). *The Bay, 1963,* is one of her most famous paintings.

"Charles Speaks of Shearer Cottage," Yvonne: The Shearer Cottage in Oak Bluffs is the oldest African American–owned inn on the Vineyard. Charles Shearer, born in Virginia in 1854, was the son of an enslaved woman and a white farm owner. When the Civil War ended, Shearer attended and later became a professor at Hampton Institute in Virginia. There he met his wife, Henrietta, also a teacher. They moved to Massachusetts in the late 1800s, attracted to the Vineyard (where a vibrant African American community was emerging), and in 1903 bought the house where Shearer Cottage is now located. The inn, which was listed in the *Negro Motorist Green Book* as a safe place to stay, is now the first stop on the African American Heritage Trail of Martha's Vineyard. It is still owned and operated by the family.

"Your Studio," Judith Herman: Helen Buchthal (1922-2013) was a painter and long-time resident of Chilmark. She was born in Germany and came with her family to London in 1938, shortly after Kristallnacht. After her education, she taught art and design. She moved to the United States in 1950 to study music at the New England Conservatory. After marriage, she and her husband, Claus, raised three children and she resumed her art studies at Manhattanville Conservatory. She earned a BFA and concentrated on her painting. After spending many summers on the Vineyard, the couple retired to Prospect Hill in Chilmark in 1991. Helen taught art and worked as a volunteer art teacher in the Vineyard School system.

"Anne Vanderhoop," Brooks Robards: When the early settlers populated Cape Cod, there were many local names that are still familiar today: Nickerson, Thacher, Rogers, Eldredge, Cahoon, Howes, Atkins, Taylor, Doane, Crowell, and Nye, among others. Vanderhoop is one such name. Anne Vanderhoop was an "Aquinnah icon" who ran the Aquinnah Shop, a food shop overlooking the Aquinnah cliffs, starting in 1941. By the late 1960s, she was fully in charge of the family business. Married to Luther Madison, the couple were famed for their pies – she'd make the crust and he would add the filling. The Vanderhoop Homestead, constructed by Edward Vanderhoop in the late 1800s, is now the Aquinnah Cultural Center.

"Gay Head," Richard Foerster: The town of Aquinnah, formerly known as Gay Head, sits on the western end of Martha's Vineyard. It is famous for its beautiful clay cliffs which were carved out by glaciers millions of years ago. (The cliffs are also unique in that they are one of the few west-facing coastlines on the East Coast.) It's also the site of Moshup Beach (also known as Aquinnah Public Beach), one of the few "clothing optional" beaches locally. The area is part of the island's Wampanoag tribe and was designated a national landmark in 1966. The current Gay Head (Aquinnah) lighthouse was built in 1852 and completed in 1856. In 2015, it was moved 120 feet due to erosion.

"Eclipses of the Heart," Robert Frazier: Maria Mitchell (1818-1889) was born and raised on Nantucket. Her Quaker parents educated her, and it was her father who stimulated her interest in astronomy and let her use his telescope. She worked as a librarian in the Nantucket Atheneum from 1836 to 1856. In October 1857, she established the orbit of a new comet, which became known as "Miss Mitchell's Comet." Her scientific achievement opened up many doors for her: she became the first woman elected to the American Academy of Arts and Sciences and, in 1850, she was elected to the American Association for the Advancement for Science. In 1865, she accepted an appointment at Vassar College as head of the observatory and professor of astronomy. She taught there until retiring in 1888 due to failing health.

"Flesh & bone as elements of time," Alix Anne Shaw: Nantucket's early settlers during the mid-seventeenth century were sheep farmers and fishermen. Although small whales sometimes came ashore during these years, it wasn't until 1690 that Nantucketers began to organize expeditions to hunt right whales. Whales were prized for their oil, and in 1715 deep-sea whaling for sperm whales began. Initially, the whales were processed on land, but once ships were able to process on board ship (in essence, becoming seagoing factories), whalers could roam the world. When oil was discovered in Pennsylvania in 1859, the demand for whale oil declined. Within ten years, the last whaling ship would sail from Nantucket. (Thom Slayter's "The Reluctant Sailor's Lament" chronicles the loneliness of the long-distance whaler, while Jarita Davis's "Nantucket Sleigh Ride" depicts the wild ride of a whaler lashed to a whale during a fierce hunt.)

Off Season: We Live Here

"In a Back Booth at Bobby Byrne's Pub," Meaghan Quinn: Starting in the early 2000s, Massachusetts experienced a rise in fatal drug overdoses, due in large part to the overprescription of opioids. Cape Cod was among the worst hit of the state's regions. In 2012, for example, it had an opiate prescription rate that was 24 percent higher than the state average, and in 2013 and 2014, more than 20 out of 1,000 people died from a drug overdose (compared to 14.7 out of 100,000 in the United States as a whole). When opiate prescriptions were dramatically restricted, users turned to heroin as a cheaper alternative. Observers have offered possible reasons for the spike in Cape Cod's drug use: some say it is because the region has a seasonal economy and year-rounders may feel isolated in the off-season, while others point to the area's higher rates of mental illness and homelessness. (Rick Smith's gritty and insightful poem "Hyannis, 1982" also highlights drug use on Cape Cod.)

ABOUT THE CONTRIBUTORS

Keith Althaus's latest book is *Cold Storage* (Off The Grid Press, 2016). He's received awards from the National Endowment for the Arts and the Massachusetts Foundation for the Arts and Humanities, and a Pushcart Prize. One of the first literary fellows at the Fine Arts Work Center in Provincetown, he lives in North Truro, Massachusetts, with his wife, Susan Baker.

Carol A. Amato has published her poetry in *the Aurorean* and *Quill's Edge Press Anthology; New Hampshire Poetry Society*, among others, and she received a Pushcart nomination in 2017. As a natural science educator, she wrote *Backyard Pets: Exploring Nature Close to Home*, a nature series published by Barron's Educational Series Inc. and Wiley & Sons.

Judith Askew's *On the Loose* won Bass River Press's first annual book award (judged by Tony Hoagland) in 2016. Three poems from a previous book, *Here at the Edge of the Sea*, were set to music by Francis Snyder, the 2018-19 composer in residence for the Cape Cod Chamber Orchestra, and performed at the orchestra's first concert.

Steven Bauer is the author of *Daylight Savings* (Gibbs Smith, 1989) which won the Peregrine Smith Poetry Prize. His poems have appeared in *The Nation, Prairie Schooner, Massachusetts Review, Chicago Review, Southwest Review*, and elsewhere. An award-winning teacher of writing, he's published six other books, including a children's book in dactylic tetrameter.

Susan Nisenbaum Becker's first book, *Little Architects of Time and Space*, was published by Word Poetry Books in 2013. A psychotherapist as well as an actor, playwright and collaborative performer with musicians and dancers, she frequently gives reading of her poems around Boston, and her work has been performed nationally and internationally.

Mary Bergman is a writer originally from Provincetown, now living on Nantucket Island. She is a contributor to NPR/WCAI's *A Cape Cod Notebook*. Her work has appeared in *McSweeney's Internet Tendency, Provincetown Arts*, and *The Common*, among others.

Susan Berlin is an eight-time Pushcart Prize nominee and two-time finalist for the National Poetry Series. She was awarded first prize in the 16th Galway Kinnell Poetry Contest by the

Rhode Island Council on the Arts. Her poetry collection, *The Same Amount of Ink*, was published by Glass Lyre Press. She lives in Yarmouth Port, Massachusetts.

Lorna Knowles Blake's first collection of poems, *Permanent Address*, won the Richard Snyder Memorial Prize from the Ashland Poetry Press and was published in May 2008. Her second collection, *Green Hill*, won the Able Muse Book Award in 2017. She divides her time between Cape Cod and New Orleans.

Winston F. Bolton is the author of *What the Air Might Say* (Rock Village Publishing, 2013) and *Among Ruins* (Cherry Grove, 2015). His work was included in college-level textbooks, *An Introduction to Literature*, 12th edition (2001), and *Literature for Composition*, 6th edition (2003), published by Addison Wesley Longman. A retired technical writer and editor, he lives in Halifax, Massachusetts.

Elizabeth Bradfield (*ebradfield.com*) is the author of four poetry collections, *Once Removed*, *Approaching Ice, Interpretive Work,* and *Toward Antarctica*, as well as *Theorem*, a collaboration with artist Antonia Contro. Her awards include a Stegner Fellowship and the Audre Lorde Prize. She lives on Cape Cod, runs Broadsided Press, works as a naturalist, and teaches creative writing at Brandeis University.

Mary-Lou Brockett-Devine is a high-school English teacher in Connecticut and works for her family's fishing business. She finds Cape Cod allows her to mix poetry with her lifetime connection to fishing and the ocean. Her poems have been published in *The Comstock Review, The Eleventh Mu*se, *Karamu*, and *Pinyon.*

J. Lorraine Brown's honors include a Vermont Studio Center Fellowship and the PNWA Zola Award. Her work has appeared in Ted Kooser's *American Life in Poetry,* NPR/WCAI's *Poetry Sunday, Broadsides on the Bus,* and many literary journals. Her poetry chapbook *Skating on Bones* (Finishing Line Press, 2011) was selected as a "Must Read" by the Massachusetts Center for the Book.

Lucile Burt is a member of the Narrow Land Poets on Cape Cod. Her poems have appeared in various journals and in the anthology *Teaching with Fire.* Her chapbook *Neither Created Nor Destroyed* (Poet's Press) won the 2012 Philbrick Poetry Prize from the Providence

Athenaeum. Her most recent book, *The Cone of Uncertainty*, was published in 2018 by Kelsay Books.

Kathy Butterworth has been a teacher, health care advocate, and shore bird ranger on Great Point. Currently, she is an advocate at A Safe Place. She has published in Nantucket with the Moors Poets Collaborative and in several journals, including *the Aurorean*, *Avocet*, *Common Ground*, *Snowy Egret* and *Mad Poets Review*.

Deirdre Callanan's *Fish Camp: North Jetty Tales* (Paper Plane Consulting, 2020) combines interviews, essays, photos, and recipes about a streetcar that has graced Casey Key, Florida, since 1946. Bass River Press awarded her its 2017 Poetry Book Prize for *Water-Dreaming*. She serves on the faculty of The Washington-Baltimore Center for Psychoanalysis.

Samm Carlton was a professional dancer in New York City and a choreographer of multi-media works. Growing up, she spent summers in a house overlooking Vineyard Sound and the islands. She is currently writing poetry and lives in Waquoit, Massachusetts.

Kathleen Casey's poetry has appeared in *How Swimmers Dream*, the *Cape Cod Times*, and online at NPR/WCAI's *Poetry Sunday* and Mass State Poetry. The natural world is a source of inspiration for this retired teacher in Falmouth, Massachusetts, who enjoys photography, gardening, birding, and music, in addition to writing and reading.

Mary Clare Casey sees the world of nature as both an inspiration and a mirror. Poetry is the vehicle that offers her an opportunity to fuse her observations and memories as well as those of others, and to serve as a reflection of the world in which we live.

Linda Haviland Conte (lindaconte.net) is the author of *Seldom Purely* (Ibbetson Street Press, 2020) and *Slow As A Poem* (Ibbetson Street Press, 2002). Her work also appears in several anthologies and magazines. She was a panelist at the Massachusetts and New Hampshire Poetry Festivals (2017). Linda is now Treasurer and Membership Coordinator for The New England Poetry Club.

Barbara Crooker is a poetry editor for *Italian Americana* and author of nine full-length books of poetry; *Some Glad Morning* was published in 2019 (Pitt Poetry Series). Her awards include the WB Yeats Society of New York Award, the Thomas Merton Poetry of the Sacred Award, and three Pennsylvania Council on the Arts Creative Writing Fellowships.

Catherine R. Cryan lives in Rhode Island and is a frequent visitor to the Outer Cape. Currently on hiatus from work as a science educator while she and her partner raise their young sons, her work has been published by *Broadsided Press, The Comstock Review, Evening Street*, and others.

Jarita Davis is a poet and fiction writer who was the writer-in-residence at the Nantucket Historical Association. She has received fellowships from the Mellon Mayes program, Cave Canem, Hedgebrook, and the Disquiet International Literary Program in Lisbon. Her collection *Return Flights* was published by Tagus Press in 2016. She lives and writes in West Falmouth, Massachusetts.

Cathie Desjardins' recent book of poems is *Buddha in the Garden* (Tasora Press, 2019), which follows her previous book, *With Child* (Tasora Press, 2008). She has been published in *Cognoscenti* and numerous journals. She teaches ongoing workshops, both privately and at Grub Street, and was Poet Laureate of Arlington, Massachusetts, from 2017 to 2019.

Susan Donnelly's newest poetry collection is *The Maureen Papers and Other Poems*. She is also the author of *Capture the Flag, Transit, Eve Names the Animals*, and six chapbooks. Widely published in journals, anthologies, textbooks, and online, Susan teaches poetry in classes and consultations from her home in Arlington, Massachusetts.

Mark Doty has published ten books of poetry, most recently *Deep Lane* (W.W. Norton, 2015), and three memoirs, including *What Is the Grass: Walt Whitman in My Life* (W.W. Norton, 2020). His honors include the National Book Award and a Whiting Writers' Award. He is a Distinguished Professor at Rutgers University and lives in New York City.

Paula Erickson, a Wellfleet washashore, is a performance artist, singer, co-founder of The Fleet Fund providing emergency assistance for Wellfleet residents, and of The Lily House, a community home for the dying. The fertile grit of life as a social worker, educator, farmer/naturalist and end-of-life doula are the fodder for her creative work.

Howard Faerstein's latest collection is *Out of Order* (Main Street Press, 2021). His poetry can be found in numerous journals, including *On the Seawall, Nine Mile, Nixes Mate, Banyan Review, Rattle, upstreet, Verse Daily* and *Connotation*. He's associate poetry editor of *CutThroat*, and lives in Florence, Massachusetts.

Alan Feldman has spent summers on the Cape since 1978 and has always kept a sailboat. While on the Cape he teaches a free drop-in workshop (begun originally with Tony Hoagland) at the Wellfleet Library. His latest book is *The Golden Coin,* 2018, winner of the Four Lakes Prize from the University of Wisconsin Press.

Frank Finale is the author of *To The Shore Once More, Volumes I-III* (Jersey Shore Books). He co-edited two poetry anthologies, *Under a Gull's Wing* and *The Poets of New Jersey,* and was poetry editor (1996 - 2012) for *the new renaissance*. He is an essayist for *Jersey Shore* magazine. His work can be found at *frankfinale.com*.

Mary Fister teaches writing and literature at the University of Hartford. Her poems have appeared in journals such as *The Massachusetts Review, Ploughshares, Tar River Poetry,* and *Volt*. Her chapbook *Provenance of the Lost* was published by Finishing Line Press in 2007. She lives in Northampton, Massachusetts, with her two kitties, a house bunny and a horse.

Richard Foerster's honors include the Discovery/The Nation Award, *Poetry* magazine's Bess Hokin Prize, a Maine Arts Commission Fellowship, the Amy Lowell Poetry Travelling Scholarship, and two National Endowment for the Arts Poetry Fellowships. His eighth collection, *Boy on a Doorstep: New & Selected Poems,* was published by Tiger Bark Press in March 2019.

Robert Frazier is a three-time winner of the Rhysling Award from the Science Fiction and Fantasy Poetry Association. His nine books of poetry include *The Daily Chernobyl* (Anamnesis Press, 2000) and *Phantom Navigation* (Dark Regions Press, 2012). He lives on Nantucket Island, where he's an oil painter and artistic director/curator for the Artists Association of Nantucket.

Brendan Galvin's nineteenth poetry collection, *Partway to Geophany,* was published by LSU Press in 2020. *Habitat: New and Selected Poems, 1965–2005* was a finalist for the National Book Award. His many other honors include a Guggenheim Fellowship, the Iowa Poetry

Prize, *Poetry*'s Levinson Prize, and two fellowships from the National Endowment for the Arts. He lives in Truro, Massachusetts.

Diane Hanna has worked as an editor, journalist, copywriter, and writing instructor. Best known for her Story Pictures©, which combine words and images for poetic effect, she believes that we make what we most need to find. She is the author of *Say It Right* and *A Book of Weather Clues*, both by Starrhill Press. She lives in Cotuit, Massachusetts.

Jeffrey Harrison's six books of poetry include *The Singing Underneath*, selected by James Merrill for the National Poetry Series in 1987, and *Between Lakes* (Four Way Books, 2020). A recipient of fellowships from the Guggenheim Foundation and the National Endowment for the Arts, he has published widely, including in *Best American Poetry, The Pushcart Prize,* and other anthologies.

Barry Hellman is a clinical psychologist whose poems appear in journals, anthologies, broadsides, and a chapbook, *The King of Newark* (Finishing Line Press, 2012). Founder of the Cape Cod Poetry Group, he curates its events and Facebook page, and designs and leads poetry workshops. He is an advisor to NPR/WCAI's *Poetry Sunday* and an Outer Cape representative for Mass Poetry.

Phyllis Henry-Jordan was born in Boston, educated at Harvard/Radcliffe, and has taught American and English literature. She has also written articles for newspapers and magazines, managed a bookstore, and done research and editing for scholars, management consultants and lawyers. She is currently Poet Laureate of the *Berkeley Times*, for which she writes a weekly poem.

Judith Herman, who spends as much time as she can on Martha's Vineyard, lives in Boston. Her chapbook *Fishing Rites* was published by West Meadow Press, a Vineyard press, and her poems have also been set to music by Glen Roven on his recent CD, *Vineyard Songs*.

Susan Horton's books include *The Reader in the Dickens World; Thinking Through Writing;* and *Difficult Women, Artful Lives,* all published by Johns Hopkins University Press. Her poetry collections include *Manual Labor, Maximal Love,* which contains poems on the Native American history of Cape Cod. An advisory editor to *The Oxford Readers' Companion to Dickens*, she is professor emerita at UMass/Boston.

Alexis Ivy is a 2018 recipient of a Massachusetts Cultural Council Fellowship in Poetry. Her first poetry collection, *Romance with Small-Time Crooks,* was published in 2013 by BlazeVOX [book]. Her second collection, *Taking the Homeless Census,* won the 2018 Editors Prize at Saturnalia Books and was published in 2020.

Terry S. Johnson was a professional harpsichordist before serving as a public school teacher for over twenty-five years. Widely published, she earned her M.F.A. in Writing from the Vermont College of Fine Arts. Her first book, *Coalescence,* won honorable mention in the 2014 New England Book Festival. Her second collection, *Plunge,* was published in 2019 by Off the Common Books.

Sean Keck is an assistant professor of English at Radford University, where he teaches American literature, creative writing, and film. His poetry and fiction appear in *Blue Earth Review, Concho River Review, Eclipse, Post Road, The Worcester Review,* and elsewhere. His family vacationed in Dennis Port for over three decades.

James W. Kershner of Cummaquid is a former newspaper reporter and editor who also taught writing at Cape Cod Community College for 25 years. He is the author of two college writing textbooks, *The Elements of News Writing* and *The Elements of Academic Writing.*

Tricia Knoll is a Vermont poet who spent many weeks in Woods Hole a few years ago. These poems are the result. Her work appears widely in journals and anthologies. Her recent collection *How I Learned to Be White* received the 2018 Indie Book award for motivational poetry.

Lindsay Knowlton, author of *Earthly Freight*, is a past recipient of fellowships from MacDowell, and the Massachusetts Artists Foundation. She won the 2021 Vermont Writers' Prize for "Death of a Barn" (*Vermont Magazine, June 2021*). Her poems have appeared in the *Boston Review, CODA, Ploughshares, Indiana Review, The Writer's Voice of the West Side Y, Nimrod,* and the *Spoon River Poetry Review.*

Alice Kociemba is the author of *Bourne Bridge* (Turning Point, 2016) and the founding director of Calliope Poetry. She was guest editor of *Common Threads*, the poetry discussion project of Mass Poetry (2015 & 2016). Alice lives in North Falmouth, Massachusetts, with her husband, Rich Youmans.

Laurel Kornhiser lived in Barnstable for forty years, where she taught at Cape Cod Community College and wrote and edited for Cape Cod magazines. Now a professor of English at Quincy College, she is a published poet and is completing her first chapbook, *Stubborn Dragonflies.*

Adeline Carrie Koscher lives on Cape Cod, where she writes as a conduit for wonder, solace, and vitality. When writing, she is the happiest person alive. Her chapbook, *Liquid Song*, also set on Cape Cod, was published in 2020. Her writing can be found in *Review Americana, The Lyon Review, Adana, Altered States, ninepatch, Zetetic,* and *Claudius Speaks.*

Stanley Kunitz (1905–2006) was the Poet Laureate of the United States, 2000 – 2001, and a recipient of the Pulitzer Prize, the Bollingen Prize, and the National Medal of Arts, among many other honors. Deeply committed to fostering community among artists, Kunitz was a founder of the Fine Arts Work Center in Provincetown and Poets House in Manhattan.

Valerie Lawson's work appears in numerous journals and anthologies. Her Resolute Bear Press published *Off the Coast Journal* and the Maine Literary Award–winning *3 Nations Anthology: Native, Canadian & New England Writers.* Formerly of Buzzards Bay, Lawson and her husband now make their home on the Downeast Maine coast.

Sara Letourneau is a poet, freelance editor, and writing coach from Foxboro, Massachusetts. She's been a frequent visitor to Cape Cod since her first birthday. Her poetry has received first place in the Blue Institute's 2020 Words on Water Contest and appeared in Mass Poetry's *Poem of the Moment, Golden Walkman Magazine, the Aurorean, The Bookends Review, Soul-Lit,* and elsewhere.

Marty Levine's poetry has been published in a variety of anthologies. A member of Ramapough Poets in the Hudson Valley, he teaches high school special education and history in the Bronx, New York. He and his family have been escaping to the Cape annually for nearly 30 years.

Diane Lockward has published four books of poetry, most recently *The Uneaten Carrots of Atonement* (Wind, 2016), and is the editor of three books about writing, most recently *The Practicing Poet: Writing Beyond the Basics.* Her poems have appeared in *Harvard Review, Southern Poetry Review, Prairie Schooner,* and others. She is the founder and publisher of Terrapin Books.

Carol Malaquias is a longtime resident of Dennis, Massachusetts, and was a teacher in the Dennis-Yarmouth district for twenty-two years. She is the author of *Kissing a Fish: Memoirs of a Fisherman's Son* (Peninsula Press, 2015), which captures her husband's memories of growing up in Provincetown.

Fred Marchant is the author of five collections of poetry, the most recent of which is *Said Not Said* (Graywolf Press, 2017). He is also the editor of *Another World Instead: The Early Poems of William Stafford,* and is co-translator (with Nguyen Ba Chung) of work by several contemporary Vietnamese poets.

Jennifer Markell's first poetry collection, *Samsara* (Turning Point, 2014), was named a "Must Read" book in 2015 by the Massachusetts Book Awards. Her work has appeared or is forthcoming in *The Bitter Oleander, Consequence, RHINO,* and *The Women's Review of Books.* Jennifer's second book of poetry, *Singing at High Altitude,* will be published by The Main Street Rag in 2021.

Gail Mazur's eight books include *Zeppo's First Wife: New and Selected Poems,* winner of the Massachusetts Book Award and finalist for the LA Times Book Prize; *Figures in a Landscape,* finalist for the National Book Award; and, most recently, *Land's End: New and Selected Poems* (2020). She is founder and director of the Blacksmith House Poetry Series in Cambridge.

Egan Millard has worked as a journalist in Alaska, Maine, and New York City, where he grew up. His poetry has been featured in *the Aurorean, The Worcester Review, Cirque,* and *Building Fires in the Snow* (University of Alaska Press, 2016), the first anthology of LGBTQ Alaskan writers. He now lives in Boston.

Donald Nitchie lives on Martha's Vineyard. He has published poems in local periodicals, *Poets of Martha's Vineyard, Cape Cod Poetry Review, Salamander,* and more. His collection *Driving Lessons* was published in 2008. He leads Poetry Drop-In on the Vineyard, using contemporary and classic poems as models or prompts for first drafts.

Mary Oliver (1935–2019) won numerous awards for poetry, including the Pulitzer Prize, the National Book Award, and a Lannan Literary Award for lifetime achievement. She held the Catharine Osgood Foster Chair for Distinguished Teaching at Bennington College until

2001. She wrote most of her twenty-seven poetry collections in Provincetown, where she lived with her life partner, Molly Malone Cook.

Rosalind Pace runs a poetry seminar at the Wellfleet Library, teaches in the summer at Provincetown Art Association and Museum (PAAM), and gathers poet-friends at her house every Sunday afternoon. She came to Truro before she knew that an ancestor settled where she now lives. She was awarded a Fellowship in Poetry from the Massachusetts Cultural Council in 2016.

Judith Partelow has lived on Cape Cod for over 40 years. Her poetry has been published in numerous compilations, and her chapbooks include *A Woman's Heart* and *Carry Me Back, A Woman's Life in Poetry*. She is also an actress, playwright, and director; her first play is titled *A Woman's Heart*. Her website is www.judithpartelow.com.

Linda Pastan's awards include the Dylan Thomas award, a Pushcart Prize, the Bess Hokin Prize from *Poetry,* the Poetry Society of America's Alice Fay di Castagnola Award, and the Ruth Lily Poetry Prize. Her books include *Carnival Evening: New and Selected Poems 1968-98* (W. W. Norton, 1999), a National Book Award finalist. She lives in Chevy Chase, Maryland.

Marge Piercy has published twenty poetry collections, most recently *Made in Detroit* and *On the Way Out, Turn Off the Light;* seventeen novels including *Woman on the Edge of Time*, *Gone to Soldiers* and *He, She and it*. She has read, lectured and given workshops in over 550 venues here and abroad. Her work is translated into 23 languages.

Meaghan Quinn is the author of *Slow Dance Bullets* (Route 7 Press, 2019). Quinn has been featured in *[PANK]*, Mass Poetry, and on NPR/WCAI's *The Point*. Her work has been published in *Salamander, Prairie Schooner, Impossible Archetype, The Puritan, Off the Coast, Adrienne, Free State Review*, and elsewhere.

Donna Razeto lives at the ocean on Cape Cod. She is still trying to find one grain of sand with her name on it.

Brooks Robards has published five volumes of poetry, most recently *Fishing the Desert* (2015), with photographer Siegfried Halus, and *On Island* (2014), with painter Hermine Hull. Recent work in anthologies and periodicals includes: *Wednesday's Poets, Island Quintet, Avocet,* the *Aurorean*, *Plainsongs*, *Fulcrum* and *Equinox*. When she's not visiting Santa Fe, NM, she lives in Northampton, MA, and summers on Martha's Vineyard.

Jennifer Rose is the author of two poetry collections, *The Old Direction of Heaven* (Truman State University Press, 2000) and *Hometown for an Hour* (Ohio University Press, 2006). A Chicago-area native, Jennifer first visited the Outer Cape in 1970, at age 11. Its landscape—especially the bay—has inspired her ever since. She lives in Waltham, Massachusetts.

Susan Jo Russell's poems have appeared in *Bellingham Review*, *Chautauqua*, *Peregrine*, *Passager*, *Slant*, *Borderlands Texas Poetry Review*, *The Comstock Review*, and elsewhere. She has twice been nominated for a Pushcart Prize and is the 2018 winner of the Amy Lowell Prize. She co-directs the Brookline Poetry Series.

Cliff Saunders grew up in Rehoboth, Massachusetts. He is the author of six chapbooks of poetry, and his poems have appeared in the *Wayne Literary Review*, *Pedestal Magazine*, *Wilderness House Literary Journal*, and *Pinyon*, among others. Now retired, he currently lives in Myrtle Beach, South Carolina.

Alix Anne Shaw (*alixanneshaw.com*) has published three poetry collections, most recently *Rough Ground: A Translation of Wittgenstein's Tractatus from Philosophy into Poetry* (Etruscan, 2018). Her collection *Undertow* (Persea, 2007) was awarded the Lexi Rudnitsky Poetry Prize. Her poems and essays have appeared in the *Harvard Review*, *Crab Orchard Review*, *Barrow Street*, *The Los Angeles Review*, and *American Poetry Review*.

Michael Shapiro retired from the frenetic world of real-estate law to write song and verse. He was a runner-up in the *Prime Time* writing contest and received an Honorable Mention in the Joe Gouveia Outermost Poetry Contest in 2017 and 2019. He resides in Brewster, Massachusetts, with his wife, Shelley, and is the father and grandfather of two.

Thom Slayter washed ashore in South Yarmouth, Massachusetts, at age ten, but then decamped to West Dennis at age 12. He is a writer, educator, and addictions counselor. His work has appeared in *The Saanich Review* and *Harvest*, and his short story "Road Fantasy" was performed as a radio play on NPR station WXEL in West Palm Beach.

Rick Smith (*docricksmith.com*) is a clinical psychologist specializing in brain damage and domestic violence; he practices in Rancho Cucamonga, California. His recent books include *The Wren Notebook* (2000), *Hard Landing* (2010), and *Whispering in a Mad Dog's Ear* (2014), all from Lummox Press. His essay "Snowed in with Carl Sandburg" appeared in the 2019 issue of *Under the Sun.*

Robin Smith-Johnson is a co-founder of the Steeple Street Poets of Cape Cod. Her book of poems *Dream of the Antique Dealer's Daughter* was published by Word Poetry in December 2013. She also published a chapbook, *Gale Warnings,* with Finishing Line Press in 2015. She lives with her family in Mashpee, Massachusetts.

Joseph Stanton's sixth book of poems is *Moving Pictures* (Shanti Arts, 2019). His poems have appeared in *Poetry, New Letters, Harvard Review, Antioch Review,* and many other journals. He has taught poetry workshops in New York City and Honolulu. He is a Professor Emeritus of Art History and American Studies at the University of Hawaii at Manoa.

David R. Surette is the author of six collections of poetry, the most recent of which are *Malden* (Moon Pie Press, 2018) and *Stable* (Moon Pie Press, 2015), the latter of which was named an Honor Book at the 2015 Massachusetts Book Awards. He lives on Cape Cod.

Maxine Susman's seven poetry collections include *Provincelands* (Finishing Line Press, 2016), set on Outer Cape Cod, and *My Mother's Medicine* (Grayson Press, 2019). Her work has appeared in *Fourth River, Paterson Literary Review, Presence, Slant, Blueline,* and elsewhere. She teaches poetry writing at the Osher Lifelong Learning Institute of Rutgers University and belongs to the poetry performance group Cool Women.

Mary G. Swope—New Yorker by birth, Cape Codder by choice and family tradition— has followed her love of language in poetry and song since childhood. She brought Revels to Washington, DC, still sings in choruses and choirs, and loves to swim in salt water. Her poems appear in a variety of publications, including *Phosphorescence* (Word Poetry, 2020).

Matthew Thorburn is the author of seven collections of poetry, including *The Grace of Distance* (LSU Press, 2019) and *Dear Almost* (LSU Press, 2016), winner of the Lascaux Prize in Collected Poetry. He lives in New Jersey with his wife and son.

Daniel Tobin has published nine books of poems, including *From Nothing* (2016), winner of the Julia Ward Howe Prize, and *Blood Labors* (2018), both with Four Way Books. His poetry has won the Discovery/The Nation Award, the Penn Warren Award, the Frost Fellowship, the Massachusetts Book Award, and fellowships from the NEA and Guggenheim Foundation, among other honors.

Sharon Tracey is the author of *Chroma: Five Centuries of Women Artists* (Shanti Arts Publishing, 2020) and *What I Remember Most is Everything* (All Caps Publishing, 2017). Her poems have appeared in *Terrain.org, The Banyan Review, SWWIM, The Ekphrastic Review*, and elsewhere. She lives in western Massachusetts and has been visiting the Cape for more than forty years.

Paula Trespas has been writing poetry for 20 years. Her poetry is observational, spanning the topics of nature, family, and loss. She retired to Yarmouth Port, Massachusetts, where her native Cape Cod became a wellspring of inspiration. She recently published a chapbook of selected poems, *Voice to Voice.*

Sarah Brown Weitzman, a past National Endowment for the Arts Fellow in Poetry and twice nominated for the Pushcart Poetry Prize, has had poems published in hundreds of journals and anthologies including *New Ohio Review, North American Review, Rattle, Verse Daily, Mid-American Review, Poet Lore, Potomac Review, Miramar, Spillway, The Antigonish Review*, and elsewhere.

Rich Youmans's work has appeared in various publications, including *Modern Haiku*, the *Cape Cod Poetry Review*, and *The Best Small Fictions* (Sonder Press, 2020). He is the editor in chief of *contemporary haibun online* and author of *Head-On: Haibun Stories* (Redbird Chapbooks, 2018). He lives in North Falmouth, Massachusetts, with his wife, Alice Kociemba.

Yvonne, the first poetry editor at feminist magazines *Aphra* and *Ms.*, is recently published in *Black in the Middle: Anthology of the Black Midwest* (Belt), *Pennsylvania English* (2020), *CV 2 – Canadian Poetry* (43.2), and *Home: An Anthology* (Flexible). Her awards include two National Endowment of the Arts grants and a Pushcart Prize. Her work can be found at *iwilla.com.*

CREDITS

Althaus, Keith. "Late Bus, Provincetown" previously published in *Harvard Review*. "From the Pilgrim Monument" previously published in *Provincetown Arts*. Copyright by Keith Althaus. Reprinted by permission of the author.

Amato, Carol A. "At Beech Forest" previously published in *Avocet, A Journal of Nature Poetry*. Copyright by Carol Amato. Reprinted by permission of the author.

Askew, Judith. Excerpt from "Orleans Parade, July 4," which was previously published in *On the Loose* (Bass River Press, South Yarmouth, MA, 2016) and *Naugatuck River Review*. Reprinted by permission of the author.

Bauer, Steven. "Marconi Station: South Wellfleet" previously appeared in *Daylight Savings* (Peregrine Smith Books, Salt Lake City, Utah, 1989) and *Massachusetts Review*. Reprinted by permission of the author.

Becker, Susan Nisenbaum. "Passionate Attraction" used by permission of the author.

Bergman, Mary. "Disappearing (Coast Guard Beach)" used by permission of the author. "Provincetown, Late October, 6 am" previously appeared on NPR/WCAI *Poetry Sunday*, April 29, 2018, titled "Late October, 6 am." Used by permission of the author.

Berlin, Susan. "At the Thrift Shop, Vineyard Haven, Christmas Eve" previously appeared in *The Same Amount of Ink* (Glass Lyre Press, Glenville, IL, 2016) and *Naugatuck River Review*. Reprinted by permission of the author.

Blake, Lorna Knowles. "On Quivett Creek" and "Washashores" previously were published in *Permanent Address* (Ashland University Press, Ashland, 2008). "Washashores" also previously appeared in *The Hudson Review*. Both poems reprinted by permission of the author.

Bolton, Winston. "A Summer Life" previously appeared in *What the Air Might Say* (Rock Village Publishing, Hingham, MA, 2013). Reprinted by permission of the author.

Bradfield, Elizabeth. "Concerning the Proper Term for a Whale Exhaling" previously appeared in *Interpretive Work* (Arktoi Books/Red Hen Press, Pasadena, 2008); reprinted by the permission of the publisher. "On the Magnetism of Certain Spots on Earth, like Provincetown," "Historic Numbers of Right Whales Skim Feeding Off Cape Cod," and "A Further Explication of Irony" previously appeared in *Once Removed* (Persea Books, New York, 2015); reprinted by permission of the publisher.

Brockett-Devine, Mary-Lou. "Blue Skies" used by permission of the author.

Brown, J. Lorraine. "Alone on Sage Pond" by J. Lorraine Brown previously appeared in *Mudfish 21*. Reprinted by the permission of the author.

Burt, Lucile. "Kayaking the Upper Pamet in May" previously appeared in *The Cone of Uncertainty* (Kelsay Books, American Fork, Utah, 2018) and in *Prime Time Cape Cod*, *Cape Cod Times*, February, 2014. "Surfcasting" previously appeared in *Neither Created Nor Destroyed* (Providence Athenaeum, Providence, RI, 2012). Reprinted by permission of the author.

Butterworth, Kathy. "No One Else is Here" used by the permission of the author.

Callanan, Deirdre. "E Is for Edward" used with the permission of the author.

Carlton, Samm. "Salt Song" previously appeared in *Spritsail*, Volume 24, Number 1, Woods Hole, 2010. Reprinted by permission of the author.

Casey, Kathleen. "The Knob at Quissett Harbor" used by permission of the author.

Casey, Mary Clare. "Fireball at the Powwow" used by permission of the author.

Conte, Linda Haviland. "Harding's Beach" previously appeared in *Seldom Purely* (Ibbetson Street Press, Somerville, MA 2020). "Chatham's Seals at South Beach" previously appeared in *Slow as a Poem* (Ibbetson Street Press, Somerville, MA, 2002). Both were reprinted by permission of the author.

Crooker, Barbara. "Eating Meltaways in Harwichport" previously appeared in *Nimrod*, 2001. Reprinted by permission of the author.

Cryan, Catherine R. "Mary Oliver, Reading" used by permission of the author.

Davis, Jarita. "Harvesting a Return" and "Nantucket Sleigh Ride" previously appeared in *Return Flights* (Tagus Press at UMass Dartmouth, Dartmouth, 2016). Reprinted by permission of the author.

Desjardins, Cathie. "Stanley's Garden" previously appeared in *Buddha in the Garden* (Tasora Books, Minneapolis, MN, 2019). Reprinted by permission of the author.

Donnelly, Susan. "Thoreau's *Cape Cod*" previously appeared in *Transit* (Iris Press, Oak Ridge, TN, 2011). Reprinted by permission of the author. "The Law Ghosts" used by permission of the author.

Doty, Mark. "Atlantis: Michael's Dream"; "Long Point Light" from *Atlantis* by Mark Doty. Copyright © 1995 by Mark Doty. Used by permission of HarperCollins Publishers.

Erickson, Paula. "Hamblen Farm Morning, Wellfleet" used by permission of the author.

Faerstein, Howard. "Provincetown" previously appeared in *Googootz and Other Poems* (Press 53, Winston-Salem, NC, 2018) and in *Aurora Poetry*. Reprinted by permission of the author.

Feldman, Alan: "I Come Back from a Sail" by Alan Feldman originally published in *A Sail to Great Island*, by Alan Feldman © 2004 by the Board of Regents of the University of Wisconsin System. Reprinted by permission of the University of Wisconsin Press. "Ashore in Oak Bluffs" originally published in *Immortality*, by Alan Feldman © 2015 by the Board of Regents of the University of Wisconsin System. Reprinted by permission of the University of Wisconsin Press.

Finale, Frank. "At the Edge of the Sea with Rachel Carson" used by permission of the author.

Fister, Mary. "Nantucket Bluff" used by permission of the author.

Foerster, Richard. "Gay Head" by Richard Foerster previously appeared in *Patterns of Descent* (Orchises Press, 1993). Reprinted by permission of the author.

Frazier, Robert. "Eclipses of the Heart" previously appeared in *Nantucket Magazine,* Spring 1998. Reprinted by permission of the author.

Galvin, Brendan. "Names by a River" previously appeared in *The Air's Accomplices* (LSU University Press, Baton Rouge, LA, 2015) and *Shenandoah,* 2011. "Pitch Pines" and "Kale Soup" previously appeared in *Habitat: New and Selected Poems, 1965 – 2005* (LSU Press, Baton Rouge, LA, 2005). "An Unsigned Postcard from Wellfleet" previously appeared in *Partway to Geophany* (LSU Press, Baton Rouge, LA, 2020) and in *Southern Review,* 2017. "Intermission" previously appeared in *The Ecopoetry Anthology,* edited by Ann Fisher and Laura-Gray Street (Trinity University Press, San Antonio, TX, 2013). Reprinted by permission of the author.

Hanna, Diane. "Roaming Around the Brewster General Store" and "For Those Who Stay" used by permission of the author.

Harrison, Jeffrey. "Returning to Cuttyhunk" previously appeared in *The Singing Underneath* (National Poetry Series, E.P. Dutton, New York, NY, 1988). Reprinted by permission of the author.

Hellman, Barry. "Leaving Provincetown" previously appeared in *The Aurorean: 20th Anniversary Issue,* 2003. "The Last Funeral Home on Nantucket" previously appeared in *The Aurorean,* 2015. Reprinted by permission of the author.

Henry-Jordan, Phyllis. "Over the Shoal, Bass River" used by permission of the author.

Herman, Judith. "Your Studio" and "Fishmonger" used by permission of the author.

Horton, Susan. "White Girl Enters Indian Lands" used by permission of the author.

Ivy, Alexis. "Booth #51 at the Wellfleet Flea Market" used by permission of the author.

Johnson, Terry S. "Brewster Cemetery" used by permission of the author.

Keck, Sean. "Sea View Playland" used by permission of the author.

Kershner, James W. "Fort Hill" used by permission of the author.

Knoll, Tricia. "Squid Jigging in Woods Hole" used by permission of the author.

Knowlton, Lindsay. "Wanting" previously appeared in *Earthly Freight* (I Universe, Bloomington, 2009). Reprinted by permission of the author.

Kociemba, Alice. "Bourne Bridge" and "Death of Teaticket Hardware" previously appeared in *Bourne Bridge* (Turning Point, a WordTech Imprint, Cincinnati, Ohio, 2016). Reprinted by permission of the author. "Her Bay" and "Homage to the *Patricia Marie*" used by permission of the author.

Kornhiser, Laurel. "Abandoned Bog, West Falmouth" used by permission of the author.

Koscher, Adeline Carrie. "Learning to Live with Water" previously appeared in *Canary: A Literary Journal of the Environmental Crisis*, Number 44, Spring 2019, and on NPR/WCAI's *Poetry Sunday*, September 25, 2016. Reprinted by permission of the author.

Kunitz, Stanley. "Route Six" copyright © 1979 by Stanley Kunitz, from *The Collected Poems* by Stanley Kunitz. Used by permission of W.W. Norton & Company, Inc.

Lawson, Valerie. "Winter Rental" used by permission of the author.

Letourneau, Sara. "At the Sandwich Glass Museum" used by permission of the author.

Levine, Martin I. "November" previously appeared in *Mercy of Tides: Poems for a Beach House* (Salt Marsh Pottery Press, Mattapoisett, MA, 2003). Reprinted by permission of the author.

Lockward, Diane. "The Properties of Light" previously appeared in *Eve's Red Dress* (Wind Publications, Nicholasville, KY, 2003). Reprinted by permission of the author.

Malaquias, Carol. "Memoirs of a Fisherman's Son" used by permission of the author.

Marchant, Fred. "Pilgrim Spring" used by permission of the author.

Markell, Jennifer. "Landscape with Painters" used by permission of the author.

ABOUT THE PUBLISHERS

Bass River Press
An imprint of the Cultural Center of Cape Cod, Bass River Press was launched in 2015 to support local poets and engage the community in the literary arts, thereby reflecting the Center's motto: All the Arts for All of Us. It typically publishes one full-length collection by a Cape or Islands poet each year but was pleased to collaborate with Calliope Poetry to publish this anthology of work by poets from both the region and far beyond its borders. For more information, email info@cultural-center.org.

Calliope Poetry
Founded in 2006 by Alice Kociemba, Calliope Poetry promotes the creation, appreciation, and celebration of poetry in all aspects of community life. For many years it ran a monthly reading series at the West Falmouth Library on Cape Cod. It has also sponsored poetry book groups, workshops, and special events featuring such renowned poets as Jorie Graham and Mark Doty. For more information, e-mail calliopepoetryforcommunity@gmail.com.

ABOUT THE COVER ARTIST

Mary Moquin, a well-known artist and teacher on the Cape, spends every summer in a remote dune cottage on Sandy Neck, where she finds most of the inspiration for her work. Her expressive paintings have won numerous awards and have been included in several regional and national juried competitions. See more of her work at marymoquin.com.